It's
Tough
Growing
Up

It's Tough Growing Up

Up

C. W. Brister

BROADMAN PRESS
NASHVILLE, TENNESSEE

ISBN: 0–8054–5311–3

Library of Congress Catalog Card Number: 79–136134
Dewey Decimal Classification: 155.5
Printed in the United States of America

To Mark

who, at nineteen, is choosing the right
steps to take on the way to maturity.
As his father and friend, I am convinced
that we have a meaningful future as
riders together on the planet earth.

Preface

You and I live in a mad moment of human history. The movement toward a new America is in process, and its outcome is uncertain. The future tide is rolling in. Will you, like a surfer, ride each wave safely—locked in the curl? Or will you be overwhelmed by change?

This is a book about growing up in a superindustrial culture. It is about your world of minirelationships with metallic people. It is about your quest for the good life, though values wither and violence flares. Without denying tough realities, this book can aid your search for a joyous, manageable life. It takes your questions and struggles seriously.

Who will we be by 1990? Restless seekers, reactionary deniers, radical revolutionaries, hopeless conformists, or victims of future shock? "I don't want to be a nobody; I want to be somebody," said a hopeful teen-ager. Yet, with culture at the breaking point, who says growing up is easy?

The highway ahead runs to meet you. It is splotched with the blood of human needs. You are bombarded with many pressures. Permanence is dead and life's pace is deadening. Yours is a transient, throw-away world of disposable people, places, and things. Families are fractured; friends are lost. The American dream has been falsified by the power of the phony and shattered by payoffs from the underworld. Debated police actions, poverty, prejudice, and pollution—all such needs challenge and simultaneously disgust people who care.

Teen-agers have watched adults long enough to conclude that life's highest purpose is to have no purpose at all. Surrounded by rock rhythms via records, tapes, and transistor radios, the world's new generation prefers nature to culture, fads to piety, action to contemplation, and revolution to history. Cultural displacement—à la Greece, Rome, and nineteenth-century Europe—is almost total. The odds against taming technology, caring amid superabundance, and achieving idealistic goals are great.

Still, you are in love with life. An occasional whiff of death, like a friend's fatal accident, is nauseating. Few things hold your world together. Words like "When you're older . . ." or "Someday . . ." no longer appease your impatient generation. You must live now—catch fistfulls of life's stuff in both hands— or miss out forever.

What—beyond music, mod styles, astrology, gurus, and intimacy—does youth value? Money? Yes, young people pump almost twenty billion dollars into the United States economy every year. Automobiles? Yes, with a set of wheels one is suddenly free from parental restraints, linked mystically with the throbbing engine's power. Sports? Travel? Dating? Protest? Sex? Freedom? Yes, all these things and more. Shifting from longtime goals, characteristic of maturity, the young person wants more and more *now*. His immediate goals are: (1) early attainment of full adult status (including sexual gratification), and (2) economic independence from parents and powerful providers. He wants to be on his own today. Such goals place a heavy burden on you and your parents.

A world youth culture is emerging. TV documentaries, student exchange programs, and personal journeys all verify that young people are much alike around the world. The same music hits record shops and radio stations almost simultaneously throughout the world. Teen-agers' favorite movies appear at theaters in Chicago, London, and Tokyo at the same time. You may not all be citified apartment dwellers, but you are urbane, unpredictable, secular, and shrewd.

The contemporary youth culture has a decidedly religious dimension, though it rejects as hypocritical any church that fails to meet human needs. Paradoxically, the higher one's ideals the more intense are his impatience and disgust with religion that rejects Christian social ministries. Some young people are turning from the established churches—subverted by apathy, status games, and political infighting—to authentic spiritual experiences and relevant service opportunities. Others are working to close "goal gaps" in local congregations.

There is no question but that there is a communication problem between young people and their over-forty parents. The generation gap is real and may become more difficult to bridge as the population shifts proportionately toward youth.

Are adolescents and adults trapped in a hopeless communication gap—"captives on the carousel of time"? My hunch is that, to survive our collision with technology, people of all ages will become convinced of the need for creative expression in the arts, life-styles, and relationships. Along with the seriousness of work we need celebrative play—what Harvey Cox, in *The Feast of Fools,* calls festivity and fantasy, else vast organizations will swallow private effort, and systems planning will erode human loving. True dialogue, with understanding of the other person in depth and with care, will enhance the prospect of survival together on earth.

Within the context of Christian faith under pressure, this book's purpose is to:

explore concerns young people feel for becoming human, involved, and responsible in an engineered environment;

clarify decisions youth makes regarding identity, vocation, and ultimate values in a time of transience; and *lift up the living realities* of faith, love, and hope that sustain youth's search for a meaningful, useful existence.

The book is addressed to students, parents, and teachers in church and public schools. Guidance counselors aiding adolescents, who wish to make sense out of life and something of themselves in society, will find wisdom here for their work. Presentation of these ideas presupposes small group discussions by healthy, growing young people.

If one wishes to make a mark upon his or her generation, he must begin with himself. To gather the pieces of your destiny, write in your own name with the title—*it's tough growing up!* This book is for someone like you.

Writing is always a shared venture. Suggestions from Hollie Atkinson, Betty Bock, Robert S. Glen, M.D., Frank E. Robinson, Ed.D., Jozie Rabyor, and Kaye Thornton—each talented in his or her own right—have strengthened this work. My wife, Gloria, and teen-age son, Mark, both encouraged the completion of this manuscript and shared in its preparation. I am also grateful to hundreds of teen-agers who, in family life conferences, have raised questions about things that matter. Their enthusiasm for life promises to all Americans a future full of hope.

C. W. BRISTER

Contents

> "What is it you want to buy?" the Sheep said at last. . . . . "I don't *quite* know yet," Alice said very gently. "I should like to look all round me first, if I might."
>
> (Lewis Carroll, *Through the Looking Glass,* 1872, Chapter 5)

1. Growing Up in a Crisis Society

Good ol' Charlie Brown of *Peanuts* fame once observed pessimistically: "The youth of this country are in bad shape." Linus, doing push-ups, counts to one hundred and discounts the gloomy observation. "I don't know about the youth, but we kids are in great shape!"

You may agree with Linus' optimistic outlook. Kids do seem to be in great shape. There are a lot of honest-to-goodness pleasures in childhood: discoveries, games, new experiences, adventures in friendship, and skills to master. Difficulties, like competition in school, gang fights in ghettos, the death of a pet, and moving to a new neighborhood serve to strengthen childish determination. Yet, some become losers at an early age.

During the kid stage you were permitted to lead a relatively carefree and independent life. If the ballet routines in Miss Addison's School of Dance were too difficult, there was always "next time, when you're a bit older."

If you missed out on Little League baseball when you were ten, your parents were reassuring: "Maybe you'll make the team next year." They had a way of encouraging you about events in everyday life: "So what? You're not playing for keeps. It's okay if you lose now and then." They tried to toughen you for achievements in school, challenges in work, and occasional scrapes with opponents. They hovered over you like a helicopter when you ran a fever, and kept you indoors on rainy days. Your world seemed simple then.

A Space of Life Between

It's difficult to say when you tire of parental protectiveness or stop your ears to advice like: "What you *should* do now. . . ." As you mature you feel (and may even say to your parents), "I wish people would stop babying me." By the time you're thirteen, you feel like speaking up in your own behalf, "I'm old enough to run my own risks now." Really, you're not ready to be completely on your own, but you want some territory, privacy, and privileges that match your new spurt of growth.

If, for example, you are the oldest of three children, your parents may have discussed certain pressures felt and privileges desired with you. They may have seen to it that you got a room of your own, and that your middle brother or sister moved down the hall with the youngest family member. On the other hand, if you had three brothers and two sisters there wasn't much space and privacy. But there were a lot of frustrations and fusses!

No two teen-agers mature at the same instant. Each person is different—following his or her own internal calendar towards maturity. This is why you resent statements that lump teen-agers into a group or treat you *en masse*. You are an individual concentrating on making a go of life, not a group with "the plague" for adults to manipulate.

Somewhere between childhood and adulthood lies adolescence when, with Charlie Brown's realism, things seem "in bad shape." It's a stage described by a fifteen-year-old boy "when things aren't funny anymore."

"Yeah," added his seventeen-year-old sister: "If you feel washed out after a day at school, and your smile feels pasted on, what is wrong? What can be done about it?" You're there when humor gives way to hurts, lonely brooding (behind closed doors) follows family quarrels, and carefree euphoria falls victim to occasional states of panic.

Part of the teen-ager's frustration is that, like the village idiot, no one takes him seriously except himself. He's the one who is hurting, yet life goes out of its way to ignore him. Take the plight of the fifteen-year-old person in American society who demands his rights. If you're under sixteen, you can't quit school, you can't work, you can't legally drive a car, you can't marry, you can't vote, you can't own property, and you can't enlist in the Army. About all that you can do (and stay out of trouble) is attend school.

A teen-ager can barely get a hearing in an adult-run environment. Who cares about Patti's complaint, "I'm always so upset about schoolwork that I feel like I'm in a state of mental collapse"? You almost have to join a chorus of voices in protest to be heard. But when that happens youth makes waves. Protests anger adults, everybody gets up-tight, and confrontations appear self-defeating.

That's why it's such a relief to find someone who understands, who puts how you feel into words. A psychiatrist expressed youth's dilemma thus: "Adolescence is schizophrenia times ten!" He meant that you live in a split-up, high-voltage, explosive situation. Inside you and outside, too, are complex situations.

The Pain Behind the Protest

Mr. or Miss In-Between is caught, like a trapeze performer suspended in flight, between dreams and someday. Adults caution the young to wait—"When you're older," and "It won't be long now." Young adventurers feel caught in a circle game, like a revolving door, that may rob them of life's chance.

Sir Winston Churchill's description of Soviet Russia also expresses the complexity of adolescence: "It is a riddle wrapped in a mystery inside an enigma." We are dealing with pain, not just complex situations, the pain of a predicament fraught with frustrations. Here is a summary of questions from my own conversations with students seeking to find out who they are and searching for a place in life.

Their concerns may help you to understand things a little better. These quotes are their realistic, actual comments.

Priorities—"How can I know which activities should take priority when there are so many demands on me?"

Pressures—"What gives parents and teachers the idea that pressuring a young person will help him 'find himself'? They push off many unnecessary responsibilities on us. We need more time just to get to know ourselves."

Money—"I need more money than the measly pittance my folks dole out each week as an allowance. Where can I get a job, besides baby-sitting, that pays more than fifty-cents an hour?"

School—"There's a lotta tension over grades at school. Also, some of the kids want more freedom—electives, smoking, freer use of facilities, and open-campus privileges. All the teachers use antique methods: lecture, take notes, homework, and regurgitate notes on exams. Learning should be discovery not a drag."

Self-evaluation—"Youth raps the System because we feel inferior. You don't have to be black to feel like a second-class citizen. We can talk all day, but who will buy our ideas? If our parents trust us, why don't they let us do a little more on our own?"

Mobility—"When you move a lot, how do you get 'in' with a church or school group of kids who have their own crowd?"

Feeling misunderstood—"Why are teen-agers blamed for everything (for instance, wrecks or fast driving)? Parents say they understand, but *do* they really? How do you get someone to like you that hates you? Why do other kids hate me?"

Family strife—"Why don't parents let us do a little more on our own? What is the best solution for tension when I can't get along with five brothers and sisters? I feel like my world's falling apart because my parents are splitting up."

Protest movements—"Why do people protest? What is gained by manifestos, draft resistance, sex parties, black liberation groups, pollution fairs, and rock festivals where drugs and free love are everywhere? Will resistance make a revolution?"

War and the Bomb—"What are your feelings on the war in Vietnam? Why do we have wars? What is their purpose? Is war essential for world peace or are there better ways of working for peace—like the U.N. and Peace Corps?"

Alcohol and Drugs—"Should a person's future be ruined by one 'trip' (LSD) or experience of smoking 'pot'? Who uses narcotics—hippies, unhappy young people, blacks, white, middle-class students? Does marijuana lead to hard drugs like heroin? Can you take drugs and still be *normal?*"

Sex and Love—"How can I know what is right or wrong concerning sex? If Christians are not supposed to go 'all the way' before marriage, how *far* can we go with a date? If sex is bad (ugly) before marriage, how does it suddenly become good (beautiful) after marriage? Why is marriage made to seem undesirable now? How will I know when I have met the right person to spend the rest of my life with?"

Doubt and uncertainty—"I wonder if I'm ever going to make my goal because there are so many hells around me."

Teen-age turmoil may subside with growth, moving toward

maturity, and the passage of time. With things happening so fast it's hard to tell "where it's at" and where it's going.

Getting Pushed to the Edge

Well before the cosmonauts had begun their flights, men wrote of being pushed aside by discoveries in the fields of geology and astronomy. Rather than being at the center of the universe, where ancient man saw himself, today's citizen feels infinitesimal. As one of several billion riders together on planet earth, you travel incognito. In one lifetime you have an opportunity to put meaning into your name, discover your place (however modest), and work with other persons for human betterment or destruction.

You might characterize youth's situation as getting pushed to the edge. Not only are you displaced by work in progress in outer space. As the current wave of protests prove, the level of hostility in America is rising. There are many adults who hate young people. Innovators feel alienated from fundamentalists of the far right. Many whites resent Negroes, and many black people hate whites. People of privilege look disdainfully upon have-nots, and there are poor who hate the wealthy. How can you avoid the either-or extremes that you detest in adults? Anger provokes resistance and the pain of growth.

Moreover, you face a speed-up in history which is sickening. Everything is changing so fast that you may find it both challenging and repulsive. You need a bridge over troubled water— some way to escape the frontier of trackless possibilities, to avoid goallessness, to stay sane in an uninhibited society.

"I've thought of several alternatives," said a student eager to have a happy, productive life, "dropping out, the Army, a radical school, or doing my best here." It is confusing! You are impatient with the status quo. Hopefully, your quest will be a fruitful restlessness, not an empty fight. You do have a great chance and constructive forces are on your side.

Prophetic persons sense the emptiness of *now* in a culture whose revolutionary forces are simultaneously technological, political, and erotic. They predict that students in the future will reject a speeded-up world that denies them meaningful contact with anybody or anything. Human transactions inflated by cybernetics, surrounded by satellites, and conducted through electric circuitry become anemic. Human associations, deprived of nutritional values, become meaningless and depressing. Depression, in turn, causes a dropout in human values. Life is cheap, faith is a fluke, and the future is a game of luck.

This book is an attempt to help you discover your bearings as earth becomes a space ship in galactic ecology. Without claiming too much it suggests:

While crises are increasing, there is more time-space between crucial situations than at first appears. All life's turning points aren't bad. Some things can be celebrated. If we "crisis-ize" mundane little matters, everything gets critical and we blow up or get sick.

You are growing up in a time of threat to traditional values. "It seems like everyone tries to use everyone else for his own pleasure," observed seventeen-year-old Anne.

"Black and white are no longer clear," Rusty added, "they just merge into a dull shade of gray." Religious rules about right and wrong are giving way to decision-making.[1] When facing a situation that can seem compromised—like cheating—teenagers once asked: "Is this right or wrong?" This book encourages you to decide matters of personal and social morality by answering questions of a different order:

—As God's person, what is authentic, what is phony for me?

—What is smart, intelligent for me in this situation?

—What is my responsibility—to God, others, self—here?

—What behavior is appropriate to someone with my values?

By asking such questions, temptations—like dropping out via alcohol, turning on with drugs, burying the System, falling victim to despair—become more than crises. They offer a time to decide who you are and where you're headed.

In an era of doubt you need to believe in someone, in worth-while concerns, and in yourself. The musical *Hair* proclaims that we are entering a new age—the Age of Aquarius—characterized by "mystic crystal revelation" and by "living dreams of vision." I doubt that we are at the dawning of the Age of Aquarius, but we need confidence to move "from faith to faith" as suggested by the Bible.

To quote the modern mystic Walter Starcke: "Whenever change takes place, faith in the old gives way to faith in the new, in things more worthy of faith." [2] You were made for faith, for trusting relationships. True, old dogmas may dismay you. Zealotry, dogmatism, and authoritarianism in any form are unappealing. You know more about what you dislike, in your limbo condition, than what you believe.

As you crawl through the sterile tunnel of studies, campus crises, and enlarging sense of world citizenship, have your eyes found a hunk of blue horizon set at the tunnel's end? Is someone tying all the bits and pieces together for you? God is there strengthening you to cope with life's heartbreaks and decisions. He will help if you ask him. One more thing.

Human relationships are endangered but can survive through tough, realistic love. Paradoxically, two revolutions are underway simultaneously in America. A "hard" revolution attacks the System on many fronts—war, poverty, pollution, violence, racism, oppression—the list becomes endless. Some young people protest enough to hurt *if* the hurt can heal.

At the same time, a "soft" revolution reshapes people toward caring, closeness, and concerned involvement. Care is the source of kindness, of human tenderness, and the opposite of apathy. The good life comes from what we care about. Charles A. Reich analyzes in *The Greening of America* (Random House, 1970) the youth culture that is turning this country toward kindness and conscience again. I share his hope for a "third phase" of consciousness—a rebirth of care.

Keeping up with all the revolutions isn't easy. The one you should not miss is today's spiritual awakening. It's the ultimate revolution. Meanwhile, you are stranded in the present.

"If a man does not keep pace with his companions perhaps it is because he hears a different drummer. Let him step to the music which he hears, however measured or far away."

(Thoreau: *Walden*)

2. Stranded in the Present

You are one of nearly thirty million teen-agers in the United States. Like other kids, you enjoy fun and games, athletic contests and winning, music with a favorite beat, money and clothes, cars and dates, travel and realistic movies. Who wants to get "aced out" of his chance at life?

The ordeal of being young isn't child's play however; it's a time of seeking to find who one is and searching for a place in life. Since each person matures at his own pace, your big problem just now is yours uniquely. Jane may feel self-conscious. She wonders: "How can I get over my shyness and become more outgoing?" Kevin may resent being lumped into the teen-age mold: "Teen-agers aren't all bad. Most of us are just trying to live day by day in a confused and mixed up world." And Debbie may know a boy she's dying to date. Her big question today is: "How am I going to get inside that lonely guy and make him ask me for a date?"

Some mid-teeners have an overweight problem, some are very poor, many are ashamed of their parents. Some fear they won't amount to much. Others wonder jealously why some lucky people have all the fun. You may feel too tall, pimply, fat, black, perplexed, poor, handicapped, or different to mix. But in one major respect you're like every other adolescent: you're stranded in the present.

You're not impressed with adult talk of World War II, the Great Depression, or the big Swing Sound of popular music in the forties. The past has had it. It seems unreal and certainly old-fashioned. Neither are you worried about where you'll live when you're forty, or if you anticipate a space trip to Mars in 1995. True, a majority of today's graduates will be entering jobs that did not exist when they were born. But things are so unpredictable that "tomorrow" seems irrelevant in your life.

What is left, of course, is the present. Today, notes psychologist Kenneth Keniston, becomes the one rock of constancy in a shifting sea of change.[3] With a slightly unreal past and an uncertain future, an intensification of today results. Admit it. You're face to face with life.

Face to Face with Life

Maybe Shakespeare was right. All the world's a stage. You are one of the players. The audience—parents, teachers, relatives, your friends—prepares to applaud your performance. You shake inside wondering, "Is this my moment?" There are doubts, "What if I blow it?" and feelings of high resolve, "But they're depending on me. I can't let them down!"

You are pressed by today's demands and tomorrow's un-certainties to live for the moment. Certain advantages of living in the present are obvious. You can travel light and be ready for anything. You are more flexible and superficially, at least, more comfortable. You owe nobody anything. You can select people as models who are real in your life now and imitate their admired qualities—clothes, hair styles, ideas, values. Problems of "cutting the apron strings" from home abound, but parents mean less and peers mean more as you grow older.

Above all, you can live today. A nineteen-year-old student, injured fatally in an automobile accident, said just before he died: "Don't cheat me God. I want to live!" You understand what he was trying to say and feel pity that he did not survive. But more, there is a strong sense that you must get maximum mileage in the present. You want to live, too.

There is another side to this out-of-dateness with the past and future however, with this increasing emphasis on the lived moment. For one thing, your self-identity is shaped in large measure from family relationships and experiences. By the time you're in senior high school a set, or life-style, has developed. If you fail to learn the meaning of maleness and femaleness, work, play, adulthood, and social membership from your mother and father, where do you discover how to be human?

Secondly, you need varied models with whom to identify. This is why friends—young and older—are crucially important. You must filter or winnow what is valuable, enduring, and worth keeping from significant others. Being selective, partial, and cautious in who you wish to be like is not easy.

You reflect the nonhero figures, film themes, and music of today, as well as the scapegoating tactics of cynical people. Who are you like or unlike in your tastes? By such a selective process you gain an ego identity—you become a real person.

Thirdly, some teen-agers, like Biff in Arthur Miller's *The Death of a Salesman,* appear unable to "take hold of life." You may know someone with so many anxieties that he doesn't know who he is or where he is going. Feelings of unrelatedness, of being adrift, of not being able to hold on to anything may be normal if they are temporary. Some of your acquaintances may appear "out of it" with drug problems, freak-out views, and notions that sound sick. Some alienated kids are sick.

Fourthly, there is danger in contemporary hedonism. The philosophy of finding pleasure in disconnected moments was expressed by a rock group leader thus: "Never have a steady job. Keep crazy hours. Get stoned. Play music. Draw constant attention, and make lots of money." Would you agree?

Jean-Paul Sartre, the French existentialist, once described the human condition of sin as life "empty of God" and lived "in bad faith" (that is, with falsehood) toward oneself and others.[4] The biblical idea of sin means essentially that one mismanages his or her life. To the degree that you discover God's purpose—your reason for living—and follow it, the happier you'll be.

I like to see young people lead responsible and satisfying lives. Success, however modest or marginal, is always more convenient and enjoyable than defeat. A search for identity can be an uncomfortable experience for students, who list anxiety and depression as persistent maladies. One way of coping with new and unfamiliar stresses is to educate oneself in what life's all about.

What's It All About?

A song "Alfie," from a movie about a playboy in the city, raises some disturbing questions about life. Do we live just for the moment? Are we meant to take more than we give? How can a young person sort it all out, pull his head together, then push ahead? How can you make sense out of life?

Those who love are characterized as "fools" by Alfie. But the songwriter has a different view: "Until you find the love you've missed, you're nothing, Alfie. . . ." Might the playboy's fun quest be a flop? Are people *its* (things) one uses then discards, or humans (thous) one cherishes in meaningful relationships? Is love awakening inside you?

There are many answers to such questions, for they are all difficult. One teen-ager told me: "Right now, I don't want to do anything like study or anything that takes real concentration except just thinking about problems, dreaming, and things of this nature. Consequently, I don't do things that I should do. I don't even try." Your problems seem private and personal—at times unanswerable.

It takes time to realize that personal doubts and anxieties are universal. To ask existential (life and death) questions is to be more human than otherwise. What pains you hurts all other teen-agers, too. Though you must solve problems on your own.

"I realize," said Jimmy, "that there are a lot of things I don't understand. I'll just have to experience them myself and suffer the consequences." You certainly would not like it if your parents took all the risks for you, all the bumps, self-doubts, and joys of discovery. You want to be free to grow, to see for yourself what it's all about.

It's about self-discovery.—Grownups think teen-agers wear funny clothes, weird hairdos, say and do strange things. There are big battles at breakfast over minor matters like Bill wearing his shirt tail outside his slacks, or wearing jeans and desert boots rather than slacks and loafers to school.

Kids talk about their battles for independence from the older generation. Their questions are really protests.

—Why do parents force us to do things against our will?

—Parents say they understand, but do they really?

—Why don't parents let us do a little more on our own, like selecting clothes and deciding on those we date?

—Our parents tell us to act our age, but why don't they treat us our age?

Haim Ginott shared seventeen-year-old Barbara's discontent,[5] "Every day I ask myself why I am not the person I would like to be. My relationship with myself is a very unhappy one. I am temperamental, a person of many moods. I pretend, so people cannot discern it. This is what I hate most about my life. I always act not like my true self.

"Fundamentally, I am a friendly person. But my teachers think that I am cold. I hate all of them so much that I just want to say, '[I reject] you superior egotistical people. I am as good as you.' When I am with people who have confidence in me, I do good work. With those who treat me as an accessory to a machine, I become stupid. All I really want of life is to have someone who can accept me as I am."

If you feel complex, angry, moody—like Barbara—don't be surprised. You're trying to figure out a lot of mysteries and to handle changes in growing up—tasks like: (1) managing sexual feelings, thoughts, dreams, fantasies; (2) removing masks of hypocrisy in order to be your authentic self; (3) thinking conceptually (that is, abstractly not just concretely as in childhood) about intellectual concerns; (4) preparing for self-sufficiency and independence once you are away from the support and guidance of parents; (5) handling differences with family members, teachers, dates, friends, and bosses on the job without blowing up; (6) internalizing your own, rather than imposed, beliefs, values, and standards of behavior; and (7) forming meaningful relationships with the opposite sex. Here, I am thinking of intimacy with another (more profound than the capacity to have sexual relations) without fear of loss of your unique self.

Part of your rebellion and your parents' response is positive. You push against those whom you love in order to test the boundaries, to determine at last who you are.

It's about costly mistakes.—We smile when someone goofs, shrugs off embarrassment, and says, "You can't win 'em all!" And you can't. One can endure minor messes. For example, Steve, visiting with his date in a friend's house, slipped on the highly polished floor, scraped the floor with his shoe heel, and fell into an expensive piece of furniture. No bones were broken. Damages to the house were minor. The worst hurt was Steve's pride.

The bigger the blunder the harder feelings and reactions are to handle. A sixteen-year-old boy who has just completed driver's education naturally wants to drive the family car on dates. If he runs a stop sign and gets smashed by a stunned adult, he's had it! Or if he careens into a child on a bicycle, and the youngster is hurt seriously, it may drive the teen-ager batty. His career as a driver is altered by experience.

It's one thing to wreck the family car on a date or shopping trip. But it's quite another to take (steal) an automobile from a parking lot and go for a fast spin with a friend. A damaged fender can be repaired, but anyone who breaks the law is asking for trouble.

Some blunders appear stupid. The fourteen-year-old boy who stowed away in the wheel cradle of a jet airliner was trying to escape a bad home situation. He attempted to cross the ocean without paying passage and obtaining a passport. Instead, he fell two hundred feet to his death when the wheel bays opened. You sense that some deeds are heroic; others tragic; some are absurd.

"I wish that I had read that book on birth control (Alan F. Guttmacher, M.D., *The Complete Book of Birth Control*) six months ago," said a beautiful, pregnant seventeen-year-old girl. She was a most unhappy person, and I was trying to help her make the most of a bitter experience. "I didn't know a thing about contraceptive products, and Al (her boyfriend) didn't use anything." Deeply depressed, she looked out the window toward the river, as though it beckoned her, and said: "Sometimes I wish I were dead!"

That young lady is happily married today. Her child was adopted by a wonderful couple. Yet emotional scars that she and her family will never outgrow remain.

We injure other persons or damage private or public property at our own risk and peril. Smoking a cigarette or drinking beer is not the same thing as setting fire to one's high school. Arsonists are treated differently by society than smokers. Laws include rebellious students.

It's about forgiveness.—Like hypocrisy, unforgiveness is a terrible load to bear. The ordeal of being young would become unbearable without forgiveness and fresh starts. If we had to pay for every error in ruinous guilt feelings, pounds of flesh, and fears of future punishment, life wouldn't be worth it.

Really, we know that life cannot be reversed nor stopped, except by death. You can never recapture childhood's innocence. Yet life need not be destroyed by one sorry episode.

A father once said: "I only hope that when John and Bill (his small sons) are grown they will say, 'Dad did his best,' and forgive my failures. Parents aren't perfect. But my errors will be mistakes of the head, not of the heart."

Holding grudges can be expensive. It can divide families, even destroy personality. We need help to get back on the track and start moving. Malcolm Boyd expressed this truth in a prayer.

It's morning, Jesus. It's morning, and here's that light and sound all over again.

I've got to move fast . . . get into the bathroom, wash up, grab a bite to eat, and run some more.

I just don't feel like it, Lord. What I really want to do is get back into bed, pull up the covers, and sleep. All I seem to want today is the big sleep, and here I've got to run all over again.

Where am I running? You know these things I can't understand. It's not that I need to have you tell me. What counts most is just that somebody knows, and it's you. That helps a lot.

So I'll follow along, okay? But lead, Lord. Now I've got to run. Are you running with me, Jesus? [6]

Stranded in the present? Making the most of today? Right! Even when you try your best—on an exam, a date, a job, in a game—you may not excel. The experience might be a flop. That's when you will want to stay in bed, pull up the covers, and have a big sleep. We learn, fortunately, even when losing. A United States manufacturer said engineers tried over 100,000 designs before perfecting a tiny flashcube. You have a legitimate complaint if parents preach instant perfection for ten minutes after you've goofed.

You need to see things in a bigger perspective to understand what you're up against. Are you old enough to run your own life, to get out of the family nest? Let's see.

> "You who can scarcely
> tolerate the old will find,
> as we have done, when
> you have come half
> circle, it becomes your
> portion to endure the
> young."
>
> (Antonina Canzoneri,
> *Letter Home,* Broadman Press, 1959)

3. Breaking Out of the Shell

Fifteen-year-old Tim's relationship to his mother and father and the world around him reflects the complicated perspective of his age. Here, we recreate a conversation after a family vacation trip to New York City and Montreal, Canada. Note Tim's rage for recognition and confusion about his state of continued dependence upon his parents.

FATHER: I would like to have gotten better acquainted with Jan (a guest who accompanied the family—also fifteen). But she slept most of the time. How do you think she enjoyed the trip, Tim?

TIM: I think she found it interesting. It was hard for her to relax around you and Mom because you're so strict on me.

MOTHER: Oh?

TIM: Yeah, you don't know how close I came to disappearing into those crowds in Greenwich Village and leaving home.

FATHER: You mean you'd take your chances with those acid-dropping "hippies" and free-loving "freaks" rather than with your relatives and friends here at home?

TIM: Well . . . Dad, you made me real mad when you forced me to get my hair cut at that creepy shop in Princeton. You really went back on your word to me that I could let it grow all summer. (*Pause*) I'm not kiddin' you. After I bought those psychedelic posters and leather sandals I was ready to cut out.

MOTHER: But something inside said: 'You need your parents'? (*He nodded.*) Also, Tim, you know that we need you.

TIM: I just wish adults would stop looking at kids on the outside. They don't really care what's on the inside. They just look at a guy's hair. If it's long, they conclude he's a freak without even knowing him.

Revolt and Conformity

Teen-age revolt and conformity are inherent in the process of becoming a person. We see the fifteen-year-old's anxious longing for understanding, feeling cut off from older people, in Tim's experience. During childhood conformity must supersede one's pulling away from parents. You may recall a semitantrum at the dinner table as you tried to speak eloquently in defense of your freedom, but your parents blocked your feelings.

To feel that no one wants you, no one cares about you, no one understands you—this is the worst kind of suffering. Unless someone recognizes you, respects your nonconformity, and permits you to do your thing, you feel alone. In fact, it can be so maddening that you feel like running away or committing suicide.

Is there any guidance for a teen-ager paralyzed by a helpless feeling of not mattering, of not really being, with other persons? What is involved in getting out of one's protective family shell and trying one's wings in free flight?

Experience has shown that this is what it's like for most young people. Freedom doesn't come all at once. Rather, you earn adulthood in several stages of development. Compare your experience with this process view of human growth.

Each child born into a family experiences three developmental phases in relation to his parents. *In childhood,* boys and girls depend upon others to make a place in the family circle for them and to provide for all their needs. Without a place and provisions secured, life is problematic. If one cannot belong to his own people, where does he fit into life? With too much conflict one is not free to grow.

During early adolescence there is reshuffling among brothers and sisters in order to find a relatively conflict-free position within the family. We should feel "at home" with our relatives, else we are "dis-eased." "I have spent some sad years with a feeling that I was not in my right place and right time," said one person. Some teen-agers leave the nest prematurely because of hunger for a conflict-free environment.

The *middle* and *late adolescent* is concerned primarily with breaking out of the protective shell provided by his parents. Tangible concerns for boys include: a driver's license, a car, military service, and continued education for a career. Late teen-age girls think especially about: finding or preparing to find a husband, along with clothes, college, and a career.

Psychologically, you should progress through three stages: (1) *dependence* upon powerful providers; (2) gaining *independence* from family attachments and controls; (3) moving from alienation to *interdependence* with parents and adults. Your parents teach you to walk, then to walk away from them as you mature. In time, given good mental health, you are able to go home again—this time, a man or woman not a child. Meanwhile there is the pain of revolt.

Breaking Out Involves Rebellion

Do you recall this complaint from our first discussion? "What gives parents and teachers the idea that pressuring a young person will help him 'find himself'? They push off many unnecessary responsibilities on us. We need more time just to get to know ourselves." When the time comes to start "cutting the apron strings" nothing that parents do or say seems right in teen-agers' eyes. The opposite may also be true.

Parents can be overbearing, even rejecting. Being kicked out if you don't get out is interpreted as family rejection. Communication (or the lack of it) becomes a problem. Sometimes parents just aren't there when you need them. As Jim said: "I can't talk to my parents. They are divorced and don't know what I feel. Neither of them is very religious. Did you have Christian parents? You were lucky. I cannot talk with them. I wish I could."

How can you work things out at home if you and your parents vibrate on different wavelengths?

One, admit your ambivalence. You have some capabilities and some limitations. You don't have to be free over night, but you're in the process of gaining freedom from family controls. You still need love, money, approval, understanding, some guidance, and encouragement from significant others.

Two, watch how you revolt. Bob Oldenburg expressed youth's longing and risks in a "Hymn to Rebellion": [7]

> Fly free, oh small sparrow.
> Be free and no one follow.
> Live free and don't ever think to return.
> Rise up, be strong, eagle.
> Cry out, be heard, oh rebel.
> Let nothing stand if it gets in your way.
> Weep not for me white dove.
> Thy plumes are blue now my love.
> And free to all who would ask for thy love.
> Flame high and scream, Phoenix,
> In pills, in acid drop kicks;
> Shot through the moon into space nothingness.

It is possible to exalt your own ego to such a degree that you lose touch with people that matter, like parents. This was

Paul's problem. He got into a fight at home and hit his mother. Later, reflecting upon the experience with a friend, Paul admitted his anger and alienation.

PAUL: The worst is yet to come, Bob. I hit mother tonight.

BOB: Paul! . . . Why? What happened?

PAUL: I just hit her, and I'm not sorry!

BOB: Back up. What happened?

PAUL: It started this morning. She started nagging me before I got up. She stormed into my room and told me to get up. I told her that my semester exams were over and that I didn't have to go to work until noon. But she made me get up anyway. (*Pause.*) As soon as I got home tonight, she jumped on my back again—just nagging.

Finally something snapped and I jumped up from the supper table and just hit her—on the shoulder.

BOB: What did your dad do?

PAUL: He did not do anything at all! (*Pause.*) Well, he told me to calm down. I started to hit him too.

BOB: What did your mother do?

PAUL: Nothing! She was too surprised.

BOB: Had you ever attacked your mother before?

PAUL: I've never hit her before, but I've hit my dad lots of times.

BOB: What would he do when you hit him?

PAUL: He would hit me back.

BOB: When did all this lick-swapping begin?

PAUL (*reflectively*): When I was thirteen and Tod was fifteen, Dad got a traveling job. He was gone a lot—sometimes two weeks at a time. We decided that we would start making our own decisions; so we did.

BOB: This is when the trouble started?

PAUL: I guess so. Mother didn't always agree with our decisions, and Dad certainly didn't agree with all of them. We were too big to whip, so he would just hit us. After awhile we started hitting him back.

BOB: What a surprise! An outsider would think you had a perfect home situation.

Anger can destroy a family, or it can become a way to show concern. Because parents and teen-agers experience a lot of tension, we will discuss anger later in some detail. Paul's experience warns us about verbal attacks, insults, and explosions. We need to express deep feelings effectively.

Three, learn to cope with overcoercion. According to psychiatrist Hugh Missildine, author of *Your Inner Child of the Past*, overcoercion is the most common parental attitude in our culture. When you were small, for example, you likely received a lot of bossing from grownups. Mother's carping still echoes in your ears: "If you'd get up ten minutes earlier you'd be on time for breakfast! Did you make your bed? It's late. Hurry! Your breakfast is getting cold. . . . Don't forget to brush your teeth. . . . You're going to be late for school!" Does that sound familiar?

You may still carry a chip on your shoulder from your "drill sergeant" father's commands: "Stand up straight. . . . I don't want to have to call you again. . . . Get off that phone! . . . Will you shut up and get to bed!"

Adults try to prove that they are good parents by constantly directing and redirecting their childrens' activities. Some mothers and fathers expect their sons and daughters to make better grades, achieve more honors, and contribute more in life than they ever did. Meanwhile, children resist coercive directions by stalling, procrastinating, daydreaming, even avoiding contact with the "drill sergeant." What can you do?

Try to see your parents' orders (suggestions, ideas) as a form of anxiety about you and their own adequacy. They don't intend to paralyze you with a daily barrage of duties. Parents need to learn how to free you for self-starts, inner directions, and accomplishments. Deciding what you really want to do and abandoning their lists of "shoulds" and "have tos" will lower your resistance and increase your self-confidence.

True, you may stir parental disapproval when you defy their directions. But you can assert your individuality (ideas, tastes, styles) without losing both parents. Excessive adult pressures are relieved as your strength and self-esteem grow. Meanwhile, we all recognize that some gaps are real.

Some Gaps Are Real!

Adults are tempted to oversimplify your struggle. "Aren't kids basically the same as we were when we came along?" a father reasoned in a parent group discussion. The answer is: "No, because today's world is not the 1940's world."

The generation gap is real.—Youth struggles for autonomy and independence. Clay wants a set of keys to his own car someday. Millie values style and wants freedom to wear her hair long and skirts short if that's the "in" look. Money is the key to the new generation's revolt. The capital of youth is *cash,* of young adulthood is *time,* and of mature adulthood is *energy.* Thus the generations' values differ.

Money liberates teen-agers who control upwards of $30 billion worth of family purchasing in addition to their own spending money. Response to questions on how teen-agers feel when shopping reveals that spending is an expression of independence. Youth buys not so much material things—cosmetics, records, cars, soft drinks, TV sets, low priced cameras —but adulthood.

You are a member of a self-contained youth society. You establish your own values, lingo, styles and skills. You enjoy liberties and luxuries that adults find hard to understand. You *are* breaking out of the shell!

The education gap is real.—Everybody's heard of the new math, new biology, new English, and new physics, but not everyone understands that an educational revolution is going on.

Today's television child, says Marshall McLuhan, author of *Understanding Media,* stays tuned to up-to-the-minute adult news—inflation, rioting, war, taxes, crime, bathing beauties, as well as to old adult movies. He learns fast from instant, *soundaroundus* communication.

Education was once restricted to Mother's lap, Father's knee, Sunday school lessons from the Scriptures, and uncomplicated primers. Learning, long associated with the glum, now is fun, action-packed, colorful, involved, and universal. The family circle has widened. Character no longer is shaped by two earnest, fumbling parents. Now all the world's a sage. Gaps of intelligence, information, and values are growing. Machines tell men what to believe, think, and do!

The communication gap is real.—My son, Mark, as a high school newspaper editor, once commented on the need for parents and teen-agers to get through to each other. He wrote:

"Today especially kids need to feel free to talk with some mature person whom they can trust. Normally you would think that this should be the parent, but it seldom is.

"Kids talk about their likes, dislikes, problems, wrongdoings, plans, desires, and loves among themselves. The reason being that they feel their parents won't understand. For the most part they are right.

"When adults look at a boy, for example, with long hair they drop him into a preselected slot—hippie, revolutionary, homo-sexual, drug user, sexually free, anti-Establishment, etc. This adult narrow-mindedness is part of the problem."

He pointed out, I think correctly, that those persons with the greatest problems come from broken homes, homes where the father or mother is consistently absent from the family circle, and from homes where parents are so strict (conservative) that the child has never really had an opportunity to be himself or herself.

What do you think of this criterion of an effective home, worded as a double question? "Do the members of your family like to go home? Having been there for a while, do they like to get out?"

The person who asked that continued: "The 'good' family is seen as one which, through its capacity for sympathetic under-standing and support, for warmth and closeness, pleasantry and fun, resolves frustrations, releases tensions, and sends its members—junior and senior—back to the bigger world again." This, of course, is the ideal.

The word "home" produces unique responses—from contempt to grateful praise—in family members. One girl recalled that her mother took her to every funeral in their small town, then expected her to look at each corpse after the service. She hated that experience; each occasion provoked resentment. It took years, plus psychotherapy, before she accepted her mother. Do you know anyone with a holdover hang-up like that?

"Home is the place where, when you have to go," wrote Robert Frost, "they have to take you in." You are lucky if home is the place where you are loved, accepted, and understood.

"For every youth and maiden who is not strictly secluded or very stupid, adolescence is a period of distressful perplexity, of hidden hypothesis, misunderstood hints, checked urgency, and wild stampedes of the imagination."

(H. G. Wells, *Joan and Peter*)

4. On Becoming a Person

Before you leave on a journey, it makes sense to consult a road map to discover different routes to your destination. If life were no more complicated than a 747 jet flight to London, a computer could do your thinking for you. During childhood you are forced to follow directions established by your parents. They keep the map and read the road signs for their children. But youth on the spot need a road map, too!

Take Matthew's experience. "Somehow I seem depressed. I don't know what I'm doing. You are always happy; you don't worry. I never see you depressed. I'm not like all these happy people around here. I can't keep up with them. What can I do? What is the cause of it?" Some young people are forced to overcome awful handicaps. Their psychological or physical suffering makes them feel different from other teen-agers.

For example, two high school seniors were talking.

RON: Do you know that Mike hasn't even applied for college? He says that he's going to Tech, but he may end up in the army if he doesn't hurry and apply somewhere.

JEAN (*in an annoyed tone*): Mike doesn't have anyone at home to back him up. How he's made it this far without someone to challenge him is more than I know. (*Pause.*) Ron, why don't you talk with him. He thinks a lot of you.

Some kids agonize without a guide. This book attempts to provide a kind of road map of the territory today's teen-agers travel. A road map is not a route. Each individual must chart his own particular course. But a map does suggest different routes one may travel to reach his objective. Thus, I cannot say in simple, self-help fashion: "This is your ticket. Follow my steps and you'll run into no difficulties." That would be dishonest. You must be free to fail or succeed.

For people who are not ashamed of having brains, here are some basic concepts to assist in charting life's travels. Feel free to discuss them with someone you trust. Part of becoming a person is breaking out of loneliness into companionship. Now, what is self-understanding all about?

No Waiting for Tomorrow

Sometimes it helps to consider the example of a bold risk-taker, like Robert F. Kennedy, who defied tragedy in his personal and political life. You may have read his reason for entering the presidential race in 1968, shortly before he was killed. "I can't be sitting around here calculating whether something I do is going to hurt my political situation in 1972. Who knows whether I'm going to be alive in 1972?" That was more than a rhetorical question.

On another occasion he said: "I think you have one time

around." Bobby Kennedy's firm religious faith and hopeful outlook forced him to speak out, even angrily, against certain social evils. Do you sympathize with his attitude voiced here?

"I think we are put here on earth to make some contribution whatever it may be. I think people should be angry enough to speak out and I think there are injustices and . . . unfairnesses in my own country and around the world, and I think that if one feels involved in it one should try to do something about it. That's what I want to do, and I don't think you can wait for a decade." [8]

Why did he go on, even after his brother, John F. Kennedy, had been assassinated? He plunged into battle against the cigarette advertisers, the automobile makers, the drug manufacturers and, ultimately, against the leader of his own party, President Lyndon Johnson. Perhaps a few words from the eulogy of Robert by his brother, Senator Edward Kennedy, will explain why he spoke out.

"Each time a man stands for an ideal, or acts to improve the lot of others, or strikes out against injustice, he sends forth a tiny ripple of hope. And crossing each other from a million different centers of energy and daring, those ripples build a current that can sweep down the mightiest walls of oppression and resistance."

It takes moral courage to try to change a world that resists corrective change. One must be secure, spiritually and emotionally, to brave society's disapproval. True, you aren't a Kennedy. But do you feel any responsibility for the burdens of the world? To feel is to care; to care is to come alive!

One thing Bobby Kennedy said strikes home—"I think you have one time around." What did he mean? Just this. We cannot afford the luxury of waiting for tomorrow. A real person must live today.

Some people die before they live. By "living today" I am not implying do anything to or with anyone, then forget the consequences. Rather, as Ross Snyder suggested in *On Becoming Human,* you can celebrate present possiblities by tuning in to

God and life now. Why wait until the world's awful problems are solved? How about coming alive to the little things—a venture worth your best, contacts with pro-life people, one conversation striking fire, a deed well done.

Anyway, you are eager to "be" someone. That's what counts.

Roots of Personal Identity

A college coed spending a holiday in Greenwich Village said to a friend, "My parents gave me everything. But they forgot one important thing. They didn't tell me who I am." You may not be college age, but if you feel that you must find out who you are then you are more human than otherwise.

When a teen-ager asks, "Who am I?" he or she is confronted with depressing complexity—the desire to know, deny, and escape oneself. The girl above, from an Ivy League campus, was becoming more aware of her identity. Life has a way of forcing each individual to integrate many emotions, impulses, memories, capacities, motives, and desires into one, whole personality.

The psychoanalyst Sigmund Freud once said: "To be completely honest with oneself is the very best effort a human being can make." It is this effort at self-honesty which we now address. Take a case in point. Two sisters, sharing the same room, only two years apart in age may react in opposite ways to the identical set of circumstances. An argument, for instance, may drive one girl to tears, while her sister immediately pursues romantic interests by telephone. Why? We react to stressful situations almost automatically in a manner learned in an earlier stage of development.

You gain identity through a life-long process. Observations of primitive and civilized persons disclose something which safeguards the continuity of an individual's development. Psychologists call this "something" human *identity*—the dynamic synthesis, at any age, of one's unique self-perceptions. Teenagers, for example, describe persons with key words, like: a swinger, sharp, a drag, with-it, out-of-it, fantastic, a bummer, neat, a zero, and so on.

Identity develops in chronological, definable stages. Erik H. Erikson has advanced a concept of eight growth tasks that must be performed from infancy to late maturity. Each task becomes a growth crisis until it is successfully completed. Adolescence, for example, provokes the crisis of the "identity formation versus identity diffusion." [9] Here is where the struggle to become a person intensifies. A two-year-old's time is taken with learning how to walk, play, and put away toys. Whereas, teen-agers are mastering harder tasks: sexual drives, school assignments, skin blemishes, part-time work schedules, dating, and so on. You are considered mature or immature according to your actions in each growth stage.

Becoming a healthy human being takes time. The decision to adopt a certain life style—mod, intellectual, surfer, black militant, protester—is seldom made all at once. You look for a hero or mini-hero to copy from competing models. You become, unconsciously, a composite of elements seen in others. Meanwhile, it's normal to have ups and downs. Perhaps you'd like all ups and no downs—an impossibility. We do reach plateaus of learning and satisfaction, however, and draw strength from placid days for stressful situations ahead.

Discover what fears you have about knowing yourself. You may have a friend who protects himself (from himself and others) by keeping his nose in a book, by working constantly, by sleeping, joking or horsing around and never being serious. "In general this kind of fear is defensive," explains psychologist Abraham Maslow, "in the sense that it is a protection of our self-esteem, of our love and respect for ourselves." [10] Conversely, someone with low self-esteem, burdensome guilt feelings, or silly fears hides his true thoughts. Hypocrisy with yourself and those around you is a heavy burden to carry.

Talking with someone who matters helps to clarify ourselves. True, as one person said, "It is not easy to bleed in the presence of another person." If, however, that listener is skilled or wise or loving, he can help. He, like a good physician, would certainly do nothing to harm you.

"Sam is a good sounding board for me," admitted Cliff. "He's more conservative than I am but he lets me try out my wild notions on him without rejecting me." This sounding-board type person may be a parent who understands, a trusted teacher who cares, or a date who admires you. In the event of acute anxiety or depression you should see a physician.

Our society has varied means—like college, technical schools, military service, even emotional illness—of granting delays to individuals who need more time before accepting adult commitments. Marriage may be a healthy or unwise "out" for some youths. One survey shows that teen-age marriages have increased 600 percent since 1940. They account for half of the 2.1 million marriages each year in the United States. Many youth marriages are known to have resulted from illegitimate pregnancy. Such couples are on shaky ground from the start.

"I'm so mixed up, I don't know what I'm saying. Do you understand what I'm trying to say?" confessed a seventeen-year-old campus beauty. She may feel numbed by disappointments at home and frightened by pressures to perform now. Here's the rub. There are so many many worries over premarital sex, the draft, jobs, alcohol, drugs, and myriads of other problems that students aren't sure of anything anymore.

You know there is no such thing as "instant maturity," but, at least, you'd like a taste of significance.

A Taste of Significance

You have a way of becoming what you cherish devotedly and and search for desperately. Right now, you may know more about what you dislike and don't want than something you do desire.

Two seventeen-year-old guys were talking about the war in Southeast Asia and the possibility of spending two to six years in military service.

TED: Hollie, did you see the list of Americans killed in Vietnam last week? Over two hundred names squeezed into a few inches of newspaper space.

HOLLIE: Yeah, I'd rather get wiped out in a highway accident than to disappear in the swamps over there. At least I might get my picture on the front page of the daily paper.

Both boys secretly longed for a taste of significance. Military service threatened to interrupt and put them on the wrong track.

Your life-style today is shaped by the legacy of yesterday, plus the promise of tomorrow. You are what you have chosen from childhood and shall choose daily in the future. There is a poignant scene in the musical *Flower Drum Song* in which the aging Chinese father Wang Chi Yang tells his son: "Almost all of what you are up to now has come from me." Wang Ta, his late adolescent son, was eager to live his own life. In the process of achieving independence, however, sparks flew between Ta and his father.

If it is any consolation to you, struggles have always occurred between the generations. Parents and teen-agers both grow in the process of maturing. Give your parents credit where it is due. You are more like them than you realize.

To repeat, you have a way of becoming what you cherish devotedly and search for desperately. What are the basic steps you will take to feel significant as a person?

Accept your physical body.—Next to your name, your body is your most prized possession. It clarifies your maleness or femaleness. Your body is a clue to how you feel about yourself —shame or pride. As your body grows and changes, you look for signs that the ugly duckling is turning into a swan. With proper diet, exercise, and health care your acne will disappear, teeth straighten, and body will gain new, graceful proportions.

Accept your sexuality.—Teen-agers are tall and short, fat and thin, black and white, but, first and foremost—you are a male or a female! Puberty, with its glandular rhythms, provokes profound physical transformations in young persons. Your attention and energies are absorbed with your "beautiful bod," as one boy put it.

Guys experience rapid alterations in physique, which lead to comparisons with friends—height, body hair, feats of strength.

Perspiration and acne concern both sexes. Overshadowing a girl's rounding hips and breasts is the onset of menstruation. A term used by some women for their menses, "the curse," tends to convey, despite humor, the notion that menstruation symbolizes the female's burden and inferior status. Such is not the case. With authentic preparation, a girl will feel proud (not ashamed) of her coming womanhood.

More or less accurate sex information becomes common knowledge at an early age—earlier than some adults imagine. Many parents are unwilling or unable to talk about sex with their growing, curious children. Some schools now instruct students in the meaning of sexual development. Books like *About Sex and Growing Up* [11] will answer many of your questions.

Form new friendships.—Boys are busy discovering a man's role in United States culture; girls are learning to accept their womanhood. Along with relationships with members of your own sex, you will search for avenues of contact with the opposite sex. One's capacity for sharing love with another person grows, often stressfully, during adolescence.

Cut some ties with your parents.—We have talked earlier about your changing relationship with your parents. You can be certain that they are experiencing "growing pains," too, as you struggle to mature. Your drive for independence and search for identity is made more difficult if your parents have only incompletely solved these problems themselves. Remember, they have parents, too! Your stormy periods may kick up old, unresolved issues in their personalities.

Search out a dependable life style.—Here, I am referring to the basic values, as well as external forms of behavior, that make you uniquely you. Life-style conscious individuals are searching constantly for models to follow. Once you have settled on the kind of person you wish to become—build an image—you fight to preserve it. Life-style's importance may be understood because it (1) commits us to a way of life; (2) communicates our identity to others; and (3) controls choices, like: subcult friends, work and play habits, religious preferences, clothing and music tastes, and other decisions.

Exercise your options as a teen-ager.—You don't have full freedom yet, but you have a lot more privileges, opportunities, and possessions than most adults had at your age. You can prove your competence as a real person by helping with family chores, getting an education, and contributing to lives around you. A nonhostile way of gaining idependence is working for pay. Another is by achieving athletic skill, mastering a hobby like woodwork, or, for a girl, learning to cook and sew.

Looking at the road map in summary, you cannot afford the luxury of waiting for tomorrow. A real person must live today. Using all available resources, identify your unique self, then opt for a taste of significance. With some help you can make it.

"Sex can ruin a beauti-
ful friendship."

   (Teen-ager Kathy
   Bottel)

5. Sex
Is Here
To Stay

W hy doesn't love make me happy?" you ask. Our romantic view of love promises pleasure to anyone who shares body and soul with a member of the opposite sex. In literature and life man appears incomplete without a woman. Why doesn't love equal happiness? In part, America's beach-and-booze crowd views sex as a commodity to enjoy freely without responsibility. A nineteen-year-old, soaking sun while sprawled by the sea in her bikini, said, "You're not worried about what you do or say here because, frankly, you'll never see these people again." [12]

On the other hand, human sexuality is not simple. Sex involves physical and soul attraction. Thus dating permits you to discover yourself in another person. Exploring the mysteries of the other sex is exciting.

You may have seen the motion picture *David and Lisa,* about two emotionally disturbed adolescents. In one scene, Lisa asks David, "What do you see when you see me?" Normal, not merely disturbed, teen-agers try constantly to find out who they are by asking, "What do other people see in me?" You catch yourself looking into other people's eyes to see your own reflection. You wonder, "Who do they think I am?"

A member of the opposite sex mirrors you, reads you, and prizes you into coming alive. When he was asked by Lisa, "What do you see when you see me?" David answered, "I see a pearl of a girl." You are like that. It isn't enough to hear yesterday's praise. You like for someone to say every day, not "I wuv everybody," but "I love you."

Teen-agers crave affection and are attracted magnetically to the opposite sex. "You know, I love to look at girls," said Dale. "Girl-watching is my biggest problem. Sometimes I think the most awful things about them. According to the Bible this is wrong. I want to get over this more than anything." But can he?

Another way to express sexuality is to admit that we cannot be human alone. Sex is here to stay. God has written maleness and femaleness into our bodies—our basic natures—and called his creation "very good" (Gen. 1:31). Contrary to what you may have been taught, sex is not bad unless it is perverted for evil purposes. God intended that sex be beautiful. Hence, personality is built or possibly destroyed through human relationships. Often, fantasies lead to perverted sexual practices.

Teen-age Sex Fantasies

I hinted in the previous discussion that there is a lot of free-floating misinformation going around about sex. A lot of teen-agers say they can discuss almost anything, except sex, with their parents. There seems to be a communications breakdown.

Some young people refrain from asking their parents questions about sex for fear of making their parents think they are experimenting. Your own idea may be to offer innocent comments on this subject, particularly if your parents can't accept the fact that their little girl or boy is growing up.

Many parents know less accurate information than their well-informed teen-agers and are threatened by sex education courses in public schools. Many think their children are too young to understand it or, if they know the "facts of life," they'll do something wrong. Parents often torture their kids by projecting flashbacks of their own guilt-laden past onto their children. One mother, suspecting that her high school sophomore daughter was "giving in" to a boyfriend, dragged her down to the family physician. The doctor did a pelvic examination, then reported: "Sue's not a virgin anymore, Mrs. Reid." Imagine Sue's relationship to her parents after that!

Myths abound. What is your attitude toward these things?

Masturbation.—I can never forget the twenty-year-old boy who was a patient in a state mental hospital. When asked what he was doing there a frown crossed his face. His explanation was a masterpiece of what old wives' tales can do. This happened to be an "old guys' tale." His father told him that, if he kept on masturbating, it would drive him crazy. Freddy thought his father was right—sex by yourself makes you mentally ill.

Medical authorities tell us that masturbation—sexual stimulation by exciting one's own genital organs—is a common practice. No one knows for sure how many boys and girls do it. Masturbation is not physically harmful; still it can unglue you. Self-stimulation of one's genitals usually provokes gratification and guilt. Such feelings may arise from the fantasies that generally accompany the act, as well as the spoken or unspoken attitudes of adults and peers that it is shameful and harmful. The practice can get out of control.

In order to clear up confusion, here are some facts you need to know.

True love grows out of healthy self-regard and generous self-giving, not uncontrollable urges. If you are preoccupied with a compulsion to stimulate yourself, it could lead to a gratification-guilt cycle that is self-defeating. Broken vows cause loss of self-respect and call for skilled help.

Sex by yourself produces mixed emotions. The act is a source of excitement and anguish to many adolescents. It often causes worry, shame, and asocial attitudes, as well as "relief." [13] When continued into marriage, it causes one's partner to feel inadequate, unable to satisfy one's neurotic sexual needs.

Masturbation is a lonely experience, not a true love relationship. Rather than relieving sexual tension there is a build-up of aggression and anxiety. Sex by yourself won't drive you crazy. Rather, it is a clue to disrupted relationships. It depletes self-esteem and bankrupts boy-girl contacts. Remember, you cannot be fully human alone.

Premarital intercourse.—Fantasies also fly around the common practice of teen-age premarital intercourse. Estimates suggest that 50 percent of United States teen-age girls are pregnant before marriage. Guys, playing the game of girl-baiting, gauge the sex market by a report in a fall issue of *Playboy*—a chart of campuses promising "Michigan girls go all the way; Baylor girls don't," and so on around the country.

Consider these fantasies suggested by psychiatrist James Malone.

Omnipotence.—This is the magical notion that you have unlimited power, that all authority rests in your decisions, and that you are "free to live and free to die" with no thought of others. Such a person has intercourse with no idea of getting stuck.

Indestructibility.—When a couple gives in and goes all the way, they think (again magically) that nothing can happen—like pregnancy and venereal disease—that love will live forever. But, as Charlie Shedd wrote in *The Stork is Dead:* Babies come from intercourse! "Most teen-agers get married because a baby is on the way." [14] Also, a girl needs to pause before losing her virginity, because boys are leery of used merchandise.

"You don't know what it's like to be depressed, scared to death, 'til you're in a home for unwed mothers," a nineteen-year-old confessed. She didn't feel indestructible.

Land of Plenty.—A movie, *The Game,* portrays free love in a land of plenty. Peter is an adolescent and a virgin. At eighteen, virginity is often a demerit pointing against a guy with so many willing girls around. The game is to prove his manhood by becoming a player—getting a girl to give in. The male ego demands that he win the argument and dominate his sex partner. Nicky, the other player, let Peter "score" on a dare. Pressured by their peer group, Peter and Nicky found more than they wanted or expected. Free love is seldom free.

There are price tags of secrecy, over-possessiveness, dishonesty. The suspicion, "Am I being used?" is always there.

Neutrality.—We have noted magical thinking among students whose distortions of reality can cause trouble. Distortions like, "I am god; nothing can happen to me; and everybody else does, why shouldn't we play, too?"

The last fantasy I shall mention is the view of sex as a neutral, uninvolving experience.

"Sex is like brushing your teeth," goes this argument, "or eating food. One should do it as much as possible to avoid harmful side effects." (Do you suppose he meant something like cavities?) Such a person avoids "commitment" in sexual experiences and views the human body as a machine. A girl's vagina is merely a convenient orifice to receive a boy's sex organ.

There's only one thing wrong with this fantasy. It isn't true! Intercourse takes on the quality of commitment, whether or not you intend it so. The eighteen-year-old girl who acknowledged, "I've used sex to hold people" is much nearer the truth. Modern females want a male who excites them, yet who cares. Wouldn't it make you feel kind of cheated to lose out on love to someone who says, "Sex is like brushing your teeth?"

Sexual relationships—secure within marriage—are fulfilling and committing. A girl never forgets "my first love," with whom she had a serious relationship. On the other hand, without love, sex can be menacing, a potential destroyer, producing extreme anxiety and guilt feelings.

Regardless of one's views on premarital intercourse, morals are changing. Some ethicists are asking, "Queen Victoria, where are you?" For good reasons we can not go back to the nineteenth-century Victorian outlook of love-without-sexuality. We are today's people.

Morals are Changing

"There are still some morals around," suggested a sixteen-year-old girl, "but they are changing." Another person in the high school group observed :"Ten years ago premarital sex was not spoken about. Now it's beginning to be something that kids are asking about. They say, 'What's wrong with premarital sex?' and they don't see anything wrong with it."

Propaganda about the new morality perverts sex as a function of the whole person. In *Playboy,* it is purely recreational; in the Kinsey reports, it is biological; and in current jokes, sex-talk is a symbol of liberation. Youth argues, "Why not?"

Round-up weekends at American university fraternities are festivals of drinking, singing and dancing, then going to bed with one, two, or more sex partners. A couple at one university in Munich, Germany, claimed a world's record for the longest kiss —one hour and forty minutes! Intercourse now embellishes teen-age courtship like a game at a birthday party. Yet, who wants to be treated like recreational equipment?

I can't say how teen-agers in general feel about premarital sexual relationships. But here is a classic insight into the subtle sexual psychology of one girl.

After intimacies with Paul, who was drafted, Shirley said, "We were all right until we got close. I don't know, but something happened. After we did it three or four times, we started fussing. Since then, we haven't cared for each other. I don't even want to see Paul when he comes home on leave."

Shirley was frightened both by the possibility of pregnancy and of rejection. A girl who violates her values is tortured by her own perception of herself as evil, by her fears of social rejection, and by her anxieties of the future. Will the same thing happen with the next guy she dates?

Contraceptives—mechanical and chemical devices to prevent conception—are readily available and widely used by unmarried persons. Psychiatrist Karl Menninger has stated that when the fear of pregnancy is removed we will have the basis for developing an authentic morality. Responsible sex experience, like true parenthood, rests not upon reducing the risks of pregnancy but sharing the relationships of married love.

It is estimated that a quarter million babies are born out-of-wedlock in the United States each year to girls under fifteen, women over forty, and all the years between. The community says, "She got pregnant," displaying a double moral standard. The fact is intercourse is an interpersonal commitment; it involves two persons in face-to-face encounter. She didn't get pregnant; they both (boy and girl) got pregnant! Conception—as well as contraception—is both the male's and female's responsibility, not the girl's alone.

Morals are changing, but the girl still gets stuck with the pregnancy, and society has a stake in the baby she bears. *Teen* magazine published this letter—a poignant cry—from a girl who learned the hard way what is involved in too-early sex. Perhaps you can learn, in advance, from her suffering.[15]

Jimmy and I couldn't wait so now we are married. Big deal!

Let me tell you what it is like to be married at 17. It is like living in this dump on the third floor up and your only window looks out on somebody else's third floor dump.

It is like coming home at night so tired you feel like you're dead from standing all day at your checker's job. But you don't dare sit down because you might never get up again and there are so many things to do like cooking and washing and dusting and ironing. So you go through the motions and you hate your job and you ask yourself, "Why don't I quit?" and you already know why. It's because there are grocery bills and drug bills and rent bills and doctor bills, and Jimmy's crummy little check from the lumberyard won't cover them, that's why!

Then you try to play with the baby until Jimmy comes home. Only sometimes you don't feel like playing with her. But even if you do, you get this awful feeling that you are only doing it because you feel guilty. She is so beautiful, and you know it isn't fair to her to be in that old lady's nursery all day long. Then you wash diapers and mix formula and you hate it, and you wonder how long it will be till she can tell how you feel, and wouldn't it be awful if she could tell already?

Then Jimmy doesn't come home, and you know it's because he is out with the boys doing the things he didn't get to do because you had to get married. So, finally you go to bed and cry yourself to sleep telling yourself that it really is better when he doesn't come because sometimes he says the cruelest things. Then you ask yourself "Why does he hate me so?" And you know it is because he feels trapped, and he doesn't love you anymore, like he said he would.

Then he comes home and he wakes you up, and he starts saying all the nice things he said before you got married. But you know it is only because he wants something, and yet you want to believe that maybe it is the old Jimmy again. So you give in, only when he gets what he wants, he turns away and you know he was only using you once more. So you try to sleep but you can't. This time, you cry silently because you don't want to admit that you care.

You lie there and think. You think about your parents and your brothers and the way they teased you. You think about your backyard and the swing and the tree house and all the things you had when you were little. You think about the good meals your mother cooked and how she tried to talk to you, but you were so sure she had forgotten what it was like to be in love.

Then you think about your girl friends and the fun they must be having at the prom. You think about the college you planned to go to, and you wonder who will get the scholarship they promised you. You wonder who you would have dated in college and who you might have married and what kind of a job would he have?

Suddenly you want to talk, so you reach over and touch Jimmy. But he is far away and he pushes you aside, so now you can cry yourself to sleep for real.

If you ever meet any girls like me who think they are just too smart to listen to anyone, I hope you'll tell them that this is what it is like to be married at 17!

Yes, there is a sex revolution in progress in our world. Some things needed to change—like men owning women as their property, like the tribe of Africans who once crucified women for committing adultery, like forcing adolescent girls to submit to a crude form of clitorectomy in order to deaden sexual response, and like circumcising boys at puberty largely to discourage masturbation. Marriages arranged by ancestors needed to go. A double standard—separate codes for men and women—should disappear from the earth.

Old appeals are gone. Yet, enduring foundations to guide sexual activity and sustain family life are needed. More than morality is involved in delaying sex until marriage.

How Do You Decide?

Christian psychologist Lofton Hudson cautions, "If we are looking in the Bible for details about sex, courtship, perversions, masturbation, incest, birth control, artificial insemination, abortion, homosexuality, and other modern problems, we will be left out in the cold." [16] Who has the answers?

What *does* the Bible say about sex and marriage? It offers enduring principles, not specific rules, about sexuality.

(1) God has written maleness and femaleness into our natures. He called his creation "very good." Thus sex is beautiful.

(2) "To know" one's mate, in the biblical sense (Gen. 4:1), implies a deep, personal relationship—a life commitment. Sex is erotic, but also involving. Intercourse becomes a covenant of communication at life's deepest level.

(3) Marriage, consummated by sexual union, needs to be entered freely—by personal selection of one's mate (Gen. 2:24). It is for the mature, who are still growing.

(4) Sexual love is holistic, not simple. This refers not only to your mate's complex mystery, but to the exclusiveness of marriage. God's intention is *one* man with *one* woman for life (Matt. 19:1–6).

(5) The ultimate ground for sexual relations is fidelity. Once selected, one's life partner merits exclusive loyalty. Husbands and

wives are dependent upon each other's faithfulness. (See Eph. 5:22–33.)

There are plain prohibitions against sex out of marriage, premarital and extramarital (Matt 15:18–20; Acts 15:19–20; I Cor. 6:18–20; I Thess. 4:3), along with the commandment: "You shall not commit adultery" (Ex. 20:14).

A conversation with sixty-two unwed mothers, ranging in age from fourteen to thirty-one, reminded me that many persons have missed the ideal mark. Many sufferers are enmeshed in tragic sex habits, in demonic perversions of true love. The Bible helps individuals whose values have been violated to find paths of foregiveness and renewal. Jesus Christ opens new ways of facing human problems and offers absolution for our sin.

"Okay," you're thinking, "sex relations belong in marriage. But that isn't going to help me know what to do on my next date. The now crowd wants sex now. They think it's silly to wait." You are correct. According to the Gallup Poll, students approve premarital sex by 2 to 1. Whereas, among persons fifty and over, 80 percent oppose sex before marriage.

You are tempted to decide sticky issues by statistics, to practice morality by instinct not by responsible decisions. Since illegitimate pregnancies abound in almost every American community, and last year more than a million American women had abortions,[17] you deserve some guidelines for premarital sexual behavior. Psychologist Evelyn M. Duvall offers three helpful bases for decision-making in *Why Wait Till Marriage?* [18] Perhaps they will help you to handle sex wisely.

One basis for deciding about sex is possible outcome.—What happens as a result of sexual relations? Something good or something bad? Your decision should be based upon possible outcome in terms of your own values. Ask: "Whom will I hurt?" A little selfishness helps: "Will it be myself?"

Another basis for moral decision is that of universality.—Ask yourself what it would be like if everyone did just what he or she felt like. If every boy took any girl who was available, what assurance would they have of fidelity after marriage? Where are the limits in a "bed now, wed later" world?

A third basis for developing premarital sex standards is cultural.—Unrestricted sex could occur only in a society (1) providing sex education in contraception; (2) where there were no prohibitions; (3) no feelings of guilt and shame; (4) if privacy were readily available; (5) if venereal diseases were rare or nonexistent; (6) where provisions were made for all illegitimate offspring; (7) where religious sanction approved premarital sex; and (8) where free love promoted family life. Such a culture, notes Duvall, is nonexistent.

"Why not?" A fourth practical idea.—Who wants to be a loser at sixteen or eighteen, a time which is already shaky enough? Virginity, despite changing attitudes, makes a girl more desirable. If you flunk on the second date, more than morality is at stake. You may lose not only your virginity but also your opportunity to marry someone you like. As Kathy said, "Sex can ruin a beautiful friendship."

To summarize, psychiatry and religion agree that men and women are made for each other. Happily, sex is here to stay. You hear a lot of fascinating, yet fictitious, stories of couples in and outside of marriage. A lot of legends are loaded with witchcraft. I call them sexual fantasies.

True, people need people all the time, everywhere. Our society provides appropriate channels for sexual expression according to one's maturity and marital state. At seventeen, it's more fun to have a date than a mate. Be true to your standards. If you're one of the many millions of American teen-agers who don't—then stop apologizing! Sex is great. Is it great enough to save for your marriage?

We need a theme? then
let that be our theme:
that we, poor grovellers
between faith and doubt,
the sun and north star
lost, and compass out,
the heart's weak engine
all but stopped, the
time timeless in this
chaos of our wills—
that we must ask a
theme, something to
think, something to say,
between dawn and
dark, something to hold
to, something to love.

(Conrad Aiken, *Time in the Rock*)

6. Discovering Your Purpose

Where are you headed in this hang-loose, gotta-have-a-gimmick world? Someone like you was described by John Lennon and Paul McCartney, of the Beatles, as "a real nowhere man." If you make it you must look out for your own future.

Getting your bearings—finding your place in adult society—may be described in one word: *tougher*. Judy Collins, in a *Life* interview (May 2, 1969), spoke for young people: "This is a crazy culture. Absolutely nutty. You see it reflected everywhere you look, this desperate search—who are we, what are we, can we ever make it in the hip world? On the scene, on the go, in the know."

As you explore the horizon of your brief span of history, you sense that the world is large enough to become lost in. "Never before," said a high school senior, "have we faced so many uncertainties. You can't count on anything staying the same." Sociologist Alvin Toffler has described the limits of human adaptability in coping with an overload of change in *Future Shock*. He warns that unless a person possesses a clear grasp of reality, clearly defined values, and priorities he or she faces big difficulties. The future shock victim experiences growing confusion and uncertainty. As the pace of change quickens, a purpose becomes imperative.

Even small victories are welcomed. A twenty-year-old secretary in a large firm came home from work one evening and sighed, "I really accomplished something today."

"Got a big job out of the way?" responded her father.

"No," she replied. "I found out that all the auditors are married." At least she knew where not to look for a date.

Becoming an adult does not free you from decisions. It increases your options and heightens the uncertainty of your future. Drugs permit only a temporary escape from reality. Whatever happened to the simple, secure world of childhood? As you search out life's options and opportunities, inevitably you will discover that everything isn't okay.

Everything Isn't Okay

You cannot live forever between twelve and twenty. Little Orphan Annie stays small for forty years only in the comic strip. Sooner or later *Winnie the Pooh* gives way to deeper things—lessons from Shakespeare, lab practicums in organic chemistry, draft board notices, auto accidents, production lines, sickness, and death.

Adulthood has a way of foreclosing on adolescence. Friends pair off and marry. Loss of family bonds leaves youth craving intimacy with someone who matters. Having a boyfriend, at eighteen, becomes desperately important for a girl. A guy can change courses or majors just so long. Eventually he must settle down and conquer a specific area of the vocational world. Can you say now, "I want to be_____"?

Ambivalence abounds. The end of adolescence is both exhilarating and depressing. According to one seventeen-year-old, "Everything isn't okay. We only stand on the edge looking over. We're ready to step into life, but not quite. It's awesome. It's pretty good. But it's terrifying! Why *do* we believe the things we were taught by our parents and the church? Is it enough just to be told what to believe?"

Teen-agers seek an authority they can trust. My son Mark expressed youth's quest: "Being a Christian is confusing. We face conflicting loyalties. For instance, all our lives our parents have taught us to 'love thy neighbor.' When we turn eighteen the United States government tries to teach us to kill our neighbors. Who is right? Whom shall we obey?" There are conflicting loyalties.

When a young person unmasks, he admits to feeling lonely, out-of-it, driven either to succeed or be conquered by life. "I don't have any big problems," said a fifteen-year-old boy, "just a lot of little ones making life bad news." He elaborated on how it is to be young—without a job, car, money, girl, or family that understands. That's a white-Anglo-Saxon-Protestant view. What about the blacks?

Psychiatrists William Grier and Price Cobbs tell in *Black Rage* what Negro youths face because of white America's assumption that black persons are stupid. A Negro youth of above-average intelligence is expected by his parents and counselors to act ignorant, stupid, and contemptible. This is white society's perception of its supremacy. It carries a high price tag of psychological expense.

The black boy wonders: "Will I be smart, clean, clever, obedient, loved, successful, important, rich (and white), or will I be stupid, dirty, awkward, defiant, despised, and an unimportant, impoverished failure (who is black)?" [19] The "promise" of education must cope with the view projected onto blacks by whites (and themselves), "Aren't they dumb niggers?" Changing humiliating prejudice is a fundamental social concern.

It's a pressure-cooker world where one can make or break it pretty fast. Another way to spell it is *trouble*.

This brings the argument around to you. Are you ready for life, but not quite? Where are you headed? Still looking for the road, or have you been fortunate enough to find it? The distance ahead looks like an immense journey, the traffic is heavy, your destination uncertain, and the time is late. Where are you headed, fast-driving man? Do you have a purpose for life?

A Purpose for Life

When asked about his work opportunity at a government installation, a high school dropout replied: "I just fell into it. I've been doing the same thing for eleven months and am bored to death. My brother-in-law's gonna get me a job in the lumberyard where he works." Without a sense of direction one is a drifter, always dependent upon someone else to think and act for him. Is the main purpose of your life to (1) get more money, (2) get married, (3) get your military service obligation out of the way, (4) "work the minimum; get the maximum," (5) leave home, (6) survive, or what?

Psychologists are generally agreed that young people work best when they have a purpose, when they understand the reasons for their work. We are all headed somewhere, searching for a passport to life. Time pushes us along. Parents and teachers pull us aside, remind us to select some goals, get on course, and keep our bearings though the world totters on the "eve of destruction."

More than a century ago Lewis Carroll pictured youth's need for purpose in *Alice's Adventures in Wonderland*. In one scene Alice speaks to the cat.

"Would you tell me, please, which way I ought to go from here?"
"That depends a good deal on where you want to get to," replied the Cat.

"I don't much care where—so long as I get *somewhere*," Alice added as an explanation.

"Oh, you're sure to do that," said the Cat, "if you only walk long enough."

Alice might be the young woman who confessed, with hands over her face, "I'm so mixed up; I don't know what I'm doing." She might be experimenting with marijuana, with sex, with cheating.

Alice, on the other hand, may be the idealist on your campus. She describes herself as "aware and concerned" about problems like war, poverty, racial inequality, hypocrisy, pollution, and the urban crisis. You may think her hangups are kind of sad. She hasn't learned that the human condition is not one of infallibility. She expects people to be perfect.

How can you find a purpose unless you know what it means? By *purpose* I imply a fundamental desire, direction of energies, and positive intention to make something of your life. A goal does not have to be stated in vocational terms, like: "I want to become an astronaut" or "I plan a modeling career." Early vocational choices may border more on fantasy than reality. Your self-expectations, life-style, and idealized image of what you desire from life are wrapped in the purpose package.

Right now, your purpose may be stated negatively. There are some things—adult deficiencies—you wish to avoid.

Michael J. Sniffen, a Princeton student just over a year ago, wrote: "A new breed of students has entered the nation's colleges . . . . They are not so much impressed with the need to earn a living as with the need to avoid the lives of quiet desperation that earning a living has forced on many of their parents. They are not so much impressed with what their parents and their nation achieved as what remains for them and their nation to do."

Managing Your Future

Some clear thinking is necessary if you and your generation escape the alternatives now jolting your parents. While trying to hang loose in deciding where to invest your life, you need a farsighted plan for the future. Otherwise, you shall become a victim, not a planner, of social change.

Short-range planning springs from and leads to more frustration. A disillusioned member of the British Parliament recently complained: "Society's gone random!"

What did he mean—that society is breaking down? Not entirely. He sensed that social policy has become erratic and hard to predict. If that is true of governments, a breakdown of decisional processes also characterizes people.

You are a now generation person, fed on the philosophy of "now-ness," of living today. You are encouraged to seek immediate payoffs and gratifications. "We're more oriented to the present," said a teen-age girl to a reporter after the mammoth Woodstock rock music festival. "It's like do what you want to do now . . . . If you stay anywhere very long you get into a planning thing . . . . So you just move on." Protest, the psychological equivalent of planlessness, has become a cardinal virtue. Burying the System is the protester's real goal.

Radicals strike a responsive doubt in sensitive persons: "Just maybe we *are* wrong." On the other hand, the unstated purpose of some protesters is to subvert democracy. They might destroy the judicial safeguards that protect them (most of all), but the rest of us as well. If yours is a "divine discontent," you'll keep the System and make it a little better. Lacking a positive purpose and plan, you could help to destroy the nation that offers you freedom to rebel.

You may have looked at life, with composer Joni Mitchell, from "both sides now," yet really don't know life at all. Thus you will keep your purpose open, fluid, sensitive to the options ahead. Add to the *desire* to make something of your life the *faith* that you can shape your future. Can you state your search for a purpose in clear terms? If not:

Open yourself to God and his will for your life.
Seek the best vocational guidance available in your school.

Find another person who needs you and be meaningful to him or her. Intimacy and identity run together in warm, human relationships. You can help each other to grow.

Discover the options open to you, as well as your basic gifts, talents, and capabilities. Life will make a place for you, but you must try to make a place for yourself.

Meanwhile, you might ask yourself:

(1) Am I just holding my ground against my parents when differences arise, or am I progressing toward definite goals?

(2) Do my parents treat me like a child because I act emotionally like a child? If I behave like a more mature teen-ager do they respect me more?

(3) Do I exercise the right to make up my own mind on some questions without interference from anyone? Do these matters receive my best judgment or spur of the moment ideas?

(4) Have I accomplished anything to be proud of this year? What recognition came when I chose responsibly?

There is a tide in the
affairs of men,
Which, taken at the flood,
leads on to fortune;
Omitted, all the voyage
of their life
Is bound in shallows and
in miseries.

(Shakespeare, *Julius
Caesar,* ACT IV, sc. 3)

7. A Time to Decide

Part of growing up is choosing the right steps to take. The day comes when you walk away from your old oxfords in a new pair of heels, wear a midi rather than a mini-length skirt, or cut your hair. Some decisions are easy; matters of conscience are harder. Deciding what to do with your life is complicated. "How can I choose my life work?" asked Bill. "There are so many things to do and that need to be done."

The time of education is upon you. Perhaps even now you throw up your hands in dismay over shaping your future. You feel powerless—living in a crowded, manipulated environment

—to control the kind of life you want when you want it. Such control, notes Fred Elder in his ecological study *Crisis in Eden* (Abingdon, 1970), is precisely what most persons cannot have.

More optimistically, your choices will affect all mankind. You are only one person but what you do affects your fellow riders on planet earth. Biophysicist Leroy Augenstein offers students an arrogant challenge: *Come, Let Us Play God* (Harper & Row, 1969)! He sees you assuming fantastic new responsibilities as one of the decisive generation. Adults can help you develop a sense of history, a decision-making apparatus, and an ethical framework within which to make needed choices—if you desire help.

There are many roads ahead: vocation, military service, college, delinquency, protest, marriage. The choice is yours. Let's look at some options as you think about your goal.

Vocation

The world of work is changing constantly. Meaningful work and play are essential to any individual's sense of well-being. You deserve the dignity and earnings of creative effort.

Young people frequently begin careers with part-time and summer job experiences. Without the seriousness of "playing for keeps," you can earn money, test likes and dislikes, and risk yourself in contacts with alien persons. At the end of the holiday period or summer vacation, you head back to school usually wiser, and maybe wealthier, for your experiences. Boys are luckier than girls in working for pay.

Possessions that income provide bring you status with your friends—a stereo set or used car, for example. Things can also compensate for psychological insecurity. One accumulates clothes, records, and other cherished status symbols in an effort to prove: "I am worthy. If you cannot accept me for what I *am,* recognize me for what I *possess.*"

I once talked with a vocational arts teacher about a steel chisel my son had forged in metal craft class. "A lot of work went into forging and grinding that piece of steel."

"Yes," he replied, "but what happened to the boy who shaped the steel is more important than the chisel itself." Here was a piece of work *he* had done. Such creative efforts fortify your sense of worth. You, not just materials, are valuable.

Caution! Everyone isn't healthy and ambitious. Mentally retarded and physically handicapped young people must depend upon parents and other sources of help. With development of aptitudes and skills some of them can be wholly or partially self-supporting. It takes courage to occupy a wheelchair.

Military Service

During an American boy's seventeenth year the anxiety of obligatory military service becomes an inescapable reality of life. His mail is flooded with postage-free envelopes, filled with messages from recruiters in various branches of the United States military establishment. He wonders: "Shall I quit school and get it over with? Is ROTC a route or a racket? If I volunteer for the Army will they let me choose what I want to do? Is there a two-year stint, rather than four or six, possible for me in the Marines?" His options are confusing.

The shackles on a young male's freedom are real! He has choices but only within limits. According to a Defense Department booklet entitled *It's Your Choice:* "Under existing laws every physically and mentally qualified male between the ages of 18½ and 26 faces an obligation to perform at least six years of military service, which may be fulfilled by various combinations of active and reserve duty." This booklet tells how to choose the branch of service that suits you best. You can obtain a free copy by writing to the Department of Defense, Washington, D. C.

As long as present laws continue, male students face some sort of military or government service. Pacifists, who oppose war or violence as a means of settling disputes and who refuse to bear arms on religious, ethical, or moral grounds, are taken seriously in light of the Supreme Court decision, June 15, 1970. It added *moral* to "religious grounds" for objecting to war.

Since details of military programs vary, it is best to inquire from informed recruiters or draft officials before making definite plans.

College

College age young people, between eighteen and twenty-four, comprise a significant percentage (about one out of nine) of the United States population. Sheer numbers—22,800,000 Americans—are impressive. About eight million youths are or have been in college, as compared with two million in 1938. Educators predict a peak enrolment above twelve million in the years just ahead. Not all high school graduates want or need to attend college. Studies reveal that about 50 percent of all students who enter United States institutions of higher learning fail to graduate. Some will prefer technical schools instead.

In addition to clues about the campus world, chapter 8 contains a discussion of college preparatory courses, new testing programs, admission procedures, tuition costs, information on government loans, and so on. The point here is that many gifted teen-agers are interested in higher education, and that hundreds of commuter campuses, private and public colleges, and universities want students.

In order to tell whether or not you are college material, test your intelligence and potential through a school guidance counselor. Published guides are available as one prepares for college entrance exams, anticipates expenses, and visits varied campuses. *College Ahead!,* written by two educators and addressed to high school students and their parents, is one such handbook.[20]

Productive options include work, military service, education, and, ultimately, marriage. But there will be large numbers of people who rebel and drop out of straight society.

Delinquency

The complexity of our highly organized society unfortunately instills a sense of helplessness and insignificance in some young people. A deprived fourteen-year-old, for example, may not understand the structure within which he lives, studies, and works. The angry youth is frustrated by his personal inability to direct life any way, to substitute something else for his limited surroundings, and to repair the system if it fails. Affluent suburban kids, on the other hand, test their parents' goodwill by tearing down, stealing, damaging, and destroying neighborhood property.

Many teen-agers have become cynical about the traditional, middle class universe. They have identified with anti-Establishment people. One seventeen-year-old boy who flunked out of high school and was subsequently dismissed from home by his crisis-torn parents, found a junked automobile by a lake and slept there for months. Some underprivileged children ransack markets, roam city streets day and night, rankle parents and police, and fight for recognition in a rapacious jungle.

There seems to be nothing to do, nowhere to go, for kids bored with apartment living and tired of the same city street. Two youths on parole from a state reformatory joined a Tuesday night church group because they had to "be somewhere" verifiable to a juvenile parole officer. Youth who take pride in "doing a job" to mock straight society find out, often too late, that their reward is a prison sentence and a blighted record for life.

Protest

Americans have grown accustomed to, though not comfortable with, seekers who drop out or resist adulthood. The hippie (freak) movement centered first in New York's East Village and in the Haight-Ashbury district of San Francisco. Now longhairs appear anywhere in the world.

"I am not a freak," said a sensitive student, reminding us that not every boy wearing long hair is a liberated radical.

While rebels are not all alike, they manifest common characteristics. Many use LSD and other hallucinogenic drugs to heighten (and distort) perception, to gain deeper insights into the inner world of feeling and consciousness. They seek love through free sexual mating, togetherness in communal living, and spiritual rebirth through aspects of Zen Buddhism, Hinduism, and Christianity.

Since they were beset by crime, police harassment, squalor, and disillusionment, many groups have dropped out of sight and developed communes in secluded wilderness areas. Members of such communal "families" speak a mystical jargon, strip themselves of city frustrations by hard work and meditation, and appear to have little connection with the realities of the world they left behind.

What have protesters taught us? There have been negative lessons about drugs, breakdown of sexual values, dirt and disease, despair and suicide. Anti-Establishment people are usually identified with affluent parents. They have asked America what lies beyond abundance. Is there a good life that transcends two cars in the garage, a respectable job, leisure time, and a good health and retirement plan? Though headed nowhere themselves, for the time being, society's dropouts have prompted pangs of conscience and soul-searching among parents, educators, politicians, and all persons in offices of authority. They are pushing us beyond fictions and oversimplified answers toward the authenticity of genuine existence.

Marriage

A survey of your options would appear incomplete without some reference to marriage. Like young men, adolescent girls are deeply involved in the search for identity, vocation, and destiny in life. Frequently, girls are torn between a personal desire to marry and establish a home and the economic necessity of finding a suitable occupation. Many who marry at an early age must work in order to supplement family income, or to support a young husband still in school who may work part-time. The stresses and strains of premature, perhaps forced, marriages are well-known. But let's be honest. Most marriages *do* make it.

Someone may be really important in your life right now. Before you marry, think about the answer to these questions. (1) Have I finished school? (2) Can I provide financially for a mate or family? (3) Am I reasonably independent of my parents? (4) Have I dated enough to know definitely the right person for me? (5) Am I ready to settle down and live with the one I love? If you answered "yes" to these questions, you may be mature enough for marriage.

Now you may be wondering about sources of information on varied problems as you search out your options.

Available Resources

Right now, as a sixteen-year-old, you're just trying to survive. Big adult decisions seem years away—when you're twenty-one.

The problem with decisions, however, is that they won't go away. Day after day, you or someone chooses the right steps to take—what to wear, who to date, which lessons come first, how much free time to goof off? The more responsible you are, thinking independently of adults, the faster you grow toward maturity. Here are daily decisions that you face:

How much to confide in your parents and what is private to keep?
Who is a fair-minded friend you can trust, share life with?
Is someone your ideal? Are you being true to your values?
Do you need a chaperon or can you be trusted anywhere?
How to say no (refuse) when you decide not to do something?

Luckily, you will not have to decide everything at once—only one thing at a time. Here is a brief list of agencies, literature, and persons who may guide your lifelong quest. Use the help that is offered.

Agencies

Public Schools usually have a guidance program of mental and vocational testing. Ask a teacher or administrator about such counseling services in your school.

Colleges and Universities provide guidance through professors assigned as advisors to individual students, campus testing programs, and occupational information. Student aid and placement services find part time employment for students and contact potential employers for graduating seniors. The health service staff members can care for health needs, including physical and mental health services.

AFL-CIO (American Federation of Labor and Congress of Industrial Organizations) provide pamphlets, periodicals, films, and a newspaper featuring labor news, job relations, and so on. AFL-CIO, 815—16th St., N.W., Washington, D. C. 20006.

U. S. Department of Labor, Washington, D. C. 20210, provides publications on job classifications, educational requirements, overseas opportunities, and pay provisions.

Chamber of Commerce of the United States, 1615 H St., N.W., Washington, D. C. 20006, provides information mainly from the perspective of management.

U. S. Employment Service operates offices in every state and provides testing, job listings, and contact with potential employers.

The Veterans Administration cooperates with the above service in providing vocational and social services for veterans.

Goodwill Industries of America, Inc., and *Services for the Blind* provide educational and employment opportunities for handicapped persons. See local telephone listings in major U. S. cities.

Service groups like the *Salvation Army, Y.M.C.A., Y.W.C.A.,* and religious Rescue Missions offer temporary housing, meals, and jobs for transient persons.

The Public Library and its branches can provide accurate occupational information. Some libraries will obtain special material when it is requested.

Personnel

Persons like school counselors, ministers, psychologists, and psychiatrists, as well as social workers, and employment agency personnel can be utilized when vocational guidance is needed. If one is chronically unhappy, absent, or restless at work, his vocational problem may be rooted in a serious emotional disorder. Failures, cutting classes, day dreaming, etc. in school are symptoms that one should seek competent help.

Literature

American Personnel and Guidance Association. *Directory of Vocational Counseling Services,* Washington, D. C.

Hoppock, Robert. *Occupational Information: Where to Get It and How to Use It in Counseling and Teaching.* New York: McGraw-Hill Book Co., 1957.

Theological, yet non-technical, statements include: Henlee Barnette, *Has God Called You?* (Nashville: Broadman Press, 1969); T. B. Maston, *God's Will and Your Life* (*Ibid.,* 1964).

U. S. Department of Labor. *Occupational Outlook Handbook.* Washington, D.C.: Superintendent of Documents; and the U. S. Employment Service, *Dictionary of Occupational Titles.* Same address.

Pinson, William M. *Resource Guide to Current Social Issues.* Waco: Word Books, 1968.

Youth has inherited a problematic world from grown-ups. You see the System's hang-ups, like: death of idealism, deeds of disruption, results of pollution, and harvest of prejudice. You see adults' blind spots, denounce militarism and war, despise crass commercialism, decry poverty and unemployment, and prefer dissent to blind patriotism. Something must be done!

Religious teen-agers wish to activate spiritual strength and denominational resources in behalf of hurt persons. They hear America's poor pleading: "Hey! Don't tell me what to believe. Show me that you care!" Youth desires deeds not words, acts of ministry not preachy dogma.

Deciding what to do about work, school, military service, and marriage is not one decision; it's a series of pressures. "How can I be certain about adult responsibilities since I have been unsuccessful in love, and other things, at seventeen?" you wonder.

I wish I could tell you, but I can't. Nobody can. The reason is that it finally comes back to the steps you take. Some things you have to decide for yourself. If you foresee college ahead, our next discussion can help you think about higher education.

> "Anybody who gets out of college having had his confidence in the perfection of existing institutions affirmed has not been educated. Just suffocated."
>
> (Al Capp, *From Dogpatch to Slobbovia,* Beacon Press, 1964)

8. What to Expect in College

A thirteen-year-old having trouble with homework is concerned with English literature in middle school, not college. Here's how it is with not-quite-with-it Eugene.

EUGENE: Oh, Mom, I have a note for you to sign. It's from Mrs. McKnight, my teacher.

MOTHER: (*Reads the note.*) Dear Mrs. F. Eugene needs a little encouragement at home to complete his English assignment. He must do his reading as well as report on major authors. Would appreciate your cooperation. May I hear from you, please. Cordially . . . .

Eugene and his mother have their work cut out for the afternoon, plus many other days. He chews on a pencil and stares into space after writing one paragraph. Grown-up pressures, like self-discipline, bother some kids. Eugene would rather ride his bike, play ball, fool around with his older brother's guitar—do anything except homework.

Does that remind you of someone you know? Perhaps you've pinned a note to your desk: "Stop wasting time; start studying." After all, getting an education is an important affair.

Not everyone elects to enroll in college or professional school. In the future, however, college enrolment will rise steadily, from the present seven million to an estimated twelve million a year. You wonder whether or not you will be one of these lucky ones. Let's assume that you will go to college at least one year. What should you expect?

Looking Ahead

How can you get a clear picture of what is happening on the American university campus? Looking at PR (public relations) materials about athletic victories and campus life? Spending a "round up" weekend in a fraternity sponsored sex party? Looking at a current catalogue of courses? Hearing students gripe about conservative administrators and stupid professors? Visiting a campus, attending classes, meeting varied teachers and students, and discovering facts for yourself?

The last idea is your best chance since each campus is unique. There is no such animal as "*the* campus mood" despite attempts by journalists to create a monolithic, interconnected image of American college campuses.

America's nearly 2,000 colleges and universities differ in size, location, sponsorship, history, financial support, intellectual climate, student mood, and faculty qualifications. While there are parallels, colleges are not identical. A campus, like a person, develops its own identity, style, and traditions. Thus educational centers are private and public, coeducational and non-coeducational, large and small, informal and traditional, modernistic and Gothic in architecture, sectarian and unrestricted in character.

"A picture . . . of which campus?" one is forced to ask. Imagine the feelings of a freshman student from Tupelo, Mississippi seeing the stately quadrangles of an Ivy League university for the first time. Put an eighteen-year-old Brooklynite on Baylor's campus, and restrictions seem like reform school.

How can you, feeling so up-in-the-air about many things, speak realistically about college? Motivation can't be dumped into someone else's lap. Here are questions that a teen-ager thinking about college should answer.

Am I college material? What if I got into some school, then flunked out? Who wants to be a failure before twenty? One's IQ (intelligence quotient) can be measured in a written or an oral test, administered by a competent counselor. But an IQ score does not measure ability accurately in all cases. One might score well above average, say 138, be a wizard in English, yet fail trigonometry.

It's smart to check your abilities and achievements with your teachers or guidance department counselor each year. During your junior year take the preliminary scholastic aptitude test administered through nationally recognized agencies like the College Entrance Examination Board and American College Testing Program. Test results will give you some idea of national test-score norms, and guide you toward an academic program meeting college requirements. You may not win a National Merit scholarship, nor graduate Phi Beta Kappa from college, but it's wise to want a good education. Be willing to work for it.

How do colleges select students? Can I be admitted with just average test scores? Are college admissions officers interested in people or test scores or both? Admissions criteria differ in private and state universities.

Colleges select students on several bases: one's high school record, test scores, personality, achievements in and outside school, and letters of recommendation from significant adults.

State schools, because of their tax-based support, screen candidates liberally. A student who is not ready for college work, however, may be placed on probation or suspended for poor academic performance.

It is important to plan ahead if you expect to attend college. Getting admitted is a process of planning and pursuing one's goal years in advance.

Getting Admitted

Which school for you? Where will you apply for admission—in one, two, or a half-dozen good schools? That all depends. "On what?" you wonder. On factors like:

1. Requirements for admission in a specific school;
2. Advantages and disadvantages of living at home and attending a commuter college;
3. What college costs (Anywhere from $500 to $4,000 a year, depending on the school you select);
4. Scholarships—academic, athletic, and other aid which might be available;
5. Learning resources—faculty strength, library tools, research facilities, cooperative ties with other campuses;
6. Pressures from parents, teachers, friends, and alumni;
7. Basic orientation—religious or secular, liberal arts or science, military or civilian, prestige or small, etc.;
8. Vocational goals and job opportunities upon graduation.

There is a right college for you, though it may not be a prestige school or the same university your parents attended.

For admission, follow application procedures listed in your school catalogue. Send proper fees, health certificate, room application, test scores, school records, and so on. If you apply at several schools, and are accepted at all of them, notify those you do not plan to attend.

Orientation sessions for new students and interested parents are usually offered during the summer months and at the start of each semester. Many questions can be answered, fears resolved, and problems avoided by determining school policies and procedures during orientation.

Coping with Campus Life

You may have seen the cartoon of a first-grade pupil, standing beside his mother, "talking" with his father who was reading the daily paper. Without looking up, the man said, "Now, your daddy won't have time to listen to what happens to you every day at school, but he definitely wants a report, a summation, if you will, when you get your college degree." One wonders if we understand growth processes at all.

In American culture, the college experience is valued as an opportunity for you to learn new social roles and skills that will prepare you for adult responsibilities. A campus—elite, prestige, or plain—offers a novel and problematic environment for growth. Your informational horizon expands, true enough, yet meaningful growth involves the entire ego. Growing up, as Marshall McLuhan says, is total.

How can one explain the elating—depressing ups-and-downs of the college world to someone who hasn't been around a university campus? It's not easy, but I can try.[21]

Students must cope successfully with six tasks in order to (1) meet social expectations, (2) maintain self-esteem and develop a sense of worth in becoming, and (3) manage emotional distress in the face of complex demands at college. These tasks include:

Learning new academic skills and competencies.—One girl said: "They require more work but it is more exciting and interesting than in high school." Let's imagine the experience of a biology student (one who misunderstood in high school Charles Darwin's long argument, *The Origin of Species by Means of Natural Selection*) upon reading in his text:

The theory of evolution is quite rightly called the greatest unifying theory in biology. The diversity of organisms, similarities and differences between kinds of organisms, patterns of distribution and behavior, adaptation and interaction, all this was merely a bewildering chaos of facts until given meaning by the evolutionary theory. There is no area in biology in which that theory has not served as an ordering principle.[22]

Reared in a conservative religious atmosphere, where divine creation by fiat was accepted unquestioningly, he may fail to distinguish theory from fact. Whose authority can he accept— God's word, his parents', or the textbook's view?

Tell this freshman that he can go *beyond* Darwin's study, since nineteenth-century man had no access to the electron microscope which aids investigation and interpretation of cellular substructures. Darwin had no basis, for example, for understanding the complex chemistry of heredity—DNA and RNA. The mystery deepens when he studies human ecology and discovers that modern evolutionary notions go beyond Darwin to the manipulation and management of the human habitat.[23] In addition to synthetic genes that may correct genetic defects, tomorrow's student will consider abortion legislation, mind and behavior manipulation, population control, and organ transplants to maintain life. Exploding fields of knowledge—from avionics to ekistics—plus new learning resources require mastery.

Developing close and meaningful friendships, as well as productive work relations, with one's peers.—Moving to a college campus permits the freshman to start with a clean slate of friends. He or she can try new relationships "on for size," pool information through informal group discussions, and clarify expectations by using upper-classmen as a sounding board for varied views.

Friendships are formed generally in two stages. Initially, one warms up and reaches out to almost any one who accepts him. It is imperative to overcome loneliness and to identify with others who are "in the same boat" when everything is new and confusing. Physical proximity—one's roommate or dormitory neighbor—usually affects first acquaintances.

Later, though one knows many people in classes, and so on, he develops deeper relationships with a few significant persons whom he calls "friends." Such ties are based on shared interests and values with a member of one's own or the opposite sex. Strivings for intimacy and identity flow together.

Dealing with physical separation from one's family and regulating one's need for autonomy and relatedness to one's parents. —When one is deeply attached to parents and home, leaving the first time for college floods him with mixed emotions. There is the freedom of being on one's own, away from mother's apron strings, delicious meals, and father's protective advice. Yet there is still the deeply felt need for economic and emotional security registered by a freshman girl: "Being here, away from home, it's up to me to decide how high I want to fly. Knowing there's still a net to catch me if I fall reassures me of many things—that net being my parents."

If one discovers that, in Thomas Wolfe's memorable phrase, he "can't go home again," where shall he turn for guidance, sympathy, value reinforcement, and affection? Likely, he will turn to friends, dates, and persons from different regional and cultural backgrounds who enrich his value system. A favorite faculty member may become an identification model. The growing student incorporates attitudes, traits (even bothersome ones), and ways of relating which he learns from others.

A fourth task is self-regulation in organizing time and activity.—Campus life demands individual initiative and organizing ability in duties as varied as learning chemistry formulas, attending chapel (in private schools), and washing soiled laundry. Pressures on a student's time are incredible.

You will soon discover that wasting time and procrastination are two common "sins" on campus. "Why do today what you can put off until tomorrow?" your "roomie" reasons. "Next week," quipped one crummy character to another in a cartoon picturing sloppiness, "we're gonna have to get organized." Have you ever felt like that?

A student enduring his first experience away from home described his depressing confusion: "It's like facing a wall one thousand miles long. Doors are everywhere, but I don't know which ones to enter and which ones to avoid."

A coed described herself as a "home-type person with a big adjustment to make" as one of 19,000 students on a state university campus.

So, how does a student survive? Through trial and error, following reliable guidance, you discipline yourself in the light of new freedoms. Watch your own calender and clock. Keep up with your checkbook and bank balance. You may feel like goofing off when there's studying to be done. With freer regulations of collegiate life, it's up to you to put first things first. Else who will come to your rescue?

Pairing off through dates, achieving intimacy with a cherished person of the opposite sex, and preparing for marriage.—Sex makes the collegiate world go 'round. Guys speak endearingly of the campus student center as "the body shop." Girl-watching becomes an ingenious hobby, often behind dark glasses. You suggest a keen place to go, and cutie's on a date.

"Harry—this guy I just met this fall—asked me out to 'dinner,' then took me to Raco's Taco Drive-in. You know how messy tacos are, rolled up, and dripping. Then he drove to the darkest part of a kind of park and stopped. Wow! Was I scared!"

All of which says—keep your head screwed on and your brains working. College sex is no light matter.

According to College Poll [24] dating, not dissent, rates number one in campus bull sessions. Males rated dates first; teachers and courses, second; sports, third; Vietnam and the draft, fourth; and campus issues, fifth.

Women students agreed with the men on the first two choices, but placed clothes third, and careers or marriage, fourth. Men and women students agreed again by rating campus issues fifth; politics, sixth; and parents and home life, seventh. How does all this sound to you? Do the bull sessions on your campus conform to the "average"?

Handling conflicts of opinion between students, faculty, and the administration.—Coming to terms with authority provokes some of youth's most dramatic, intense struggles. At home, the individual runs into varied adult reactions—indifference, domination, fraternizing, scapegoating, even outright rejection. One high school senior, Kathryn Ann, said that she was just "living to get away from home." You may know some individual who "waited out" high school in order to gain his or her independence.

Adults, however, have the last laugh. Most of them have lived long enough to discover how illusory freedom can be. There is enough of your parents in you, because of early identifications and later positive and negative modeling, so that your "independence" actually becomes a reliving of early experiences in all later relationships. This explains your delight with certain faculty members and anxiety in the presence of others. For some (unconscious) reason, you dislike a pushy professor who reminds you of an aggressive parent, or you identify with a profane person who "tells off" authority figures in his lectures. In rejecting the existing moral, social or political order, he speaks for you.

Sitting there reading this, you can think of rules which, because they are conservative in your judgment, you oppose. How can you appropriately show your dissatisfaction—complaining privately, rebelling against the chancellor, dropping out of college? Have you examined the politics of dissent? Protests on United States campuses parallel youth rebellion in other countries. Likely no campus will escape the reality of dissent, the pressure of activists and demonstrators, in years to come. Since "student power" is a national issue, what lies behind it? Having some answers can be an asset.

> "When youth gets skeptical, I submit, it does not indicate that anything is wrong with youth, but rather that something is wrong with adults. . . . The point is this: Adults often like to pretend the real world does not exist. Kids cannot. We might want to *escape* from it, but we cannot *forget* about it."
>
> (Harvard student Steven Kelman, "You Force Kids to Rebel," *Adolescence for Adults,* 1969)

9. Staying Sane on Campus

Inevitably some of the backwash from students rebelling at other schools will reach your campus. Problems worse than boredom, noisy dorms, and freshman depression can hit. "Worse than that stuff they call 'food' in the cafeteria?" you ask.

Kids may outgrow the generation gap. But *skepticism,* a profound loss of faith in the System, infects students at the bone marrow level. This is the disillusionment with ideas taught from childhood. "The evidence grows," said a nineteen-year-old, "that the *real* world and the world being taught us are not the same." Some students never rebel; most do get depressed.

"It gets pretty depressing to watch what is going on in the world and realize that your education is not equipping you to do anything about it," said a college senior.[25] Was she on a picket line demonstrating against some social or campus issue— a rebel protesting some radical cause? No, she will graduate with honors, and profound disillusionment, feeling that her liberal arts education isn't relevant.

Will feelings like that go away from America's schools in the future? Two English lawyers, both Oxford graduates, hurriedly visited with students from Harvard to Berkeley, at the time of the Free Speech Movement, then wrote in *A Short Walk on the Campus* that unrest would be short-lived. In light of several significant studies of student activism, it is likely that collegians will be trying to overcome campus and social ills for years to come.[26]

What's Behind Dissent?

Since the Free Speech Movement at Berkeley in the fall of 1964, student dissent has become a national issue. Many students participating in demonstrations fail to understand fundamental causes of campus unrest. Friends of four Kent State University students, killed in 1970 by National Guardsmen, claimed that they were watching the student-Guard showdown, *not* leading it. Dissent is brutal, risky business. It affects everyone—administrators, faculty, students, and the public.

Each year marks a new, significant turn in the campus crisis. Why? Because the university provides a sensitive barometer to social change in America. Old local issues, like student sharing in curriculum planning and black studies programs, are giving way to national problems: war, prejudice, pollution, and the break up of white-Anglo-Saxon-Protestant values. Causes of dissatisfaction vary, but campus ferment is widespread.

Who leads the protests? *Newsweek* (June 15, 1970) sees leadership passing from the revolutionary New Left to less violent liberals and moderates. In 1968, a Harris poll showed the activist population to be less than 2 percent of those in college.[27] Less than 1 percent pay dues to the radical SDS (Students for a Democratic Society). If the transformation now engulfing our schools continues, a significant portion of American college students will engage in political action in the future.

Perhaps the campus scene would not have caused so much concern if the press had not reported it so thoroughly. The mass media tend to magnify gaps in authority, religious values, morality, and political credibility. Television reporters and film makers have been furiously attentive to the young.

While an open confrontation may not occur on your campus, revolutionary experiences are happening in the academic world. Would you label these facts "causes" or "evidences" of campus turmoil? Think of the multi-faceted, sometimes irrational, incidents that *trigger* student dissent and civil disobedience:

1. Worldwide student unrest—Bogota, Tokyo, Prague, Paris, etc.;
2. The assassinations of idealists like John and Robert Kennedy and Martin Luther King, Jr.;
3. Message songs from rock groups, Bob Dylan, and others;
4. Permissiveness of the new morality (situation ethics);
5. Military draft and involvement in the Vietnam war;
6. Conflagrations flowing from "black power" protests; and
7. A sickening sense that the American dream might never become a reality for millions of United States citizens.

Like a rock dropped into a placid pool, toss any of these incendiary issues onto any combustible campus and agitation is sparked. Administrators can no longer "go it alone" in meeting overt protests based upon such realistic issues. Nor can they avoid the reality of student politics.

The Student's Situation

Adults have not always understood the reality of the student's situation. What it means to be a student today, note Stanford professors Joseph Katz and Nevitt Sanford, is "not yet sufficiently vivid in the minds of administrators and faculty, even those who hold positions of special responsibility for students." [28] Calling for sympathetic appreciation of the high degree of integrity which most college students possess, they suggest facets of campus life like:

1. An academic setting where students are herded into classrooms in which any sense of participation in the learning process is minimal;

2. Dormitory life offers little privacy. It, the student may conclude, is a noisy, oppressive, unwanted community;

3. Doubts about identity, adequacy, vocation, faith, his parents' values, and guilt over personal failures;

4. Profound struggles over sexual roles and behavior;

5. And, for men, the omnipresent shadow of the draft and a war whose meaning many persons deeply question.

Into each life some rain must fall. True. But in college raindrops appear preliminary to bombshells bursting everywhere. You may feel: "This campus is *so* impersonal, and I'm a zero."

America is the only country, noted Negro educator Arthur Lewis of Princeton, where students are required "to fritter away their precious years in meaningless" walking about from subject to subject "spending twelve weeks getting some tidbits of religion, twelve weeks learning French, twelve weeks seeing whether the history professor is stimulating, twelve weeks seeking entertainment from the economics professor, twelve weeks confirming that one is not going to be able to master calculus." [28] Part of student unrest lies just here. He doubts that core and cafeteria-type courses in a typical curriculum will fit him for life.

Consider an insider's perspective of the student situation. Here are excerpts from a letter by a state university coed.

School today was absolutely horrible. I woke up with a sore throat, it was raining and to top it all off, I had fever. But I had to go to my classes, especially one which I had not attended yet.

My first class was a Zoology lecture. Let me clue you in now that I'm a flat zero when it comes to science. So, picture if you will, an auditorium filled with 400 "eager" students, ready with pen in hand to take an hour's worth of good notes. Now, picture a prof, with a microphone hanging from his neck, standing 50 feet away. I suppose he's a good prof although no one is able to make out one word he says. Granted, you can hear and understand all the articles—small words like *a, the,* and *an*—ones you've heard all your life. BUT: he has the worst case of mumbling I've ever heard. People leave cursing him, his voice, plus the fact we all leave knowing as much as when we entered.

I don't know what I'm going to do. I can just picture myself exclaiming, "Listen, would you like to see 400 pupils get something out of your class? Then speak distinctly!"

So much for Zoology 101, but not for the unforgettable lessons that Mary learned in that educational establishment. Is mumbling grounds for gripes or should she stage a riot?

Inexperienced students find it difficult to distinguish serious from recreational dissent. All assaults on the system are not identical. One of the most popular games being played is "Let's Protest." Players do not wish to get involved in heavy, significant issues, but being popular demands that they do something. Panty raids are games; protests are more explosive.

Protest Is No Plaything

Sensitive Christians on campus cannot hide in a library or laboratory foxhole. You have to face the flak, survive, and accomplish goals along with tough-minded activists. You may be the conscientious objector to war or participant in civil disobedience—not "the others." Idealistic fantasies of becoming a "campus savior" may provoke you to dissent.

The Christian cannot initiate protest and, when it gets out of hand, say: "I'm washing my hands of this mess." The student who seeks to integrate a church near campus needs to care whether or not his actions "blow" the congregation. He needs to answer the question, "Before God—why am I doing this?"

"Protest," notes David L. McKenna, president of Seattle Pacific College, in Washington, "is no plaything. This is the lesson that must be learned above all others. . . . Even nonviolent protest is potentially a dangerous weapon that can escalate out of control of the protesters and . . . of the college." [30] This administrator discovered that the postmortem of a college comes when youth lose their trust in adults and when adults lose hope in youth.

While full fraternal equality among students, faculty, and administration appears a fanciful wish at this juncture, some lessons have been learned from the politics of dissent. *One,* we need to understand things from the paying customers' (students and parents) perspectives. A student's feelings about and attitudes toward his situation are real. *Two,* in addition to sensitivity, there is the need for patient negotiation of realistic and responsible solutions to adult-youth differences. A parley of working partners beats a protest any day! *Three,* schools need to enlarge the opportunities for the students' own choices. A range of options in curriculum, campus rules, living provisions, and off-campus study programs should enhance, not threaten, the maturing process.

Finally, "the college student of 1980," [31] and the indefinite future, will be moving in the direction pointed to by the student activists described above—toward a better, freer, more human existence.

Living with Student Unrest

A college education is revolutionary. Outside and inside, many forces are at work. You may feel that you are being "put together" properly in your undergraduate or professional school program. Despite sounds of unrest and an uneasy spirit, you are gaining facts, skills, and wisdom that secure your personal identity, social position, and economic status in the future. You are turning a corner, maturing in college.

On the other hand, there will be days when dark thoughts flood your entire being. You may think that you're about to crack up or go out of your skull. As one guy put it:

All of a sudden, I'm not *sure* anymore—not sure I want to be a lawyer—not sure I'm ready to marry Sandi—not even sure I really belong in college. Maybe if my folks would stop *hounding* me! . . .

Who decided I wanted to be a lawyer, anyway? If I could just drop out for a while . . . . I don't know how much more I can take! [32]

Wellsprings of anxiety flood the young person's mind during acutely stressful times.

When you are not sure *who* you are and *where* you're heading, it's time to let some trusted person in on your problem. Find a faculty advisor, adult friend, mature student, or campus counselor with whom you can talk in complete confidence.

Religious faith points you to the stars of hope and peace even on cloudy, dark nights of the soul. You may not have all the answers, but faithfulness to God *is* an act of faith. You can be true to the spiritual light you have. Books like my *Dealing With Doubt* (Broadman Press, 1970) help in troubled times.

Any successful life is marked by small victories over growth problems and pressure points along the way. As Graham Blaine, Jr. and Charles McArthur, of the Harvard University Health Services, point out in *Emotional Problems of the Student,* some anxieties are temporary. Tensions connected with studying and dating can usually be relieved by rest, physical exercise, change of pace, and self-discipline. Day-to-day disturbances are most easily ameliorated during the period of their emergence.

Paralyzing problems—like basic character disorders, sex deviance, dependence on drugs or alcohol, and acute depression —require differential diagnosis and treatment in safe medical hands. Thus, when emotional disturbances hang on and won't go away through routine methods of tension release, check with the college health service for expert aid. Relieved of excessive anxiety, the student is ready for work again.

"College provides some of the happiest, most exciting times of one's life," said a graduating senior. "It also involves one in agonizing crises and tragic hurts. The University was the greatest experience of my life."

Perhaps you have *been there*. You know about homesickness,

the time squeeze, rejection, pride, and the secret sadness of having been disloyal to life's highest loyalties. You may never have participated in public protest, but you know a lot about private gripe sessions. You've learned the risks of magic (unrealistic) thinking, disappointment of an empty mail box, and depression over a flat wallet.

At your best, however, you're glad for the excitement of learning. To be awed at how great life is, to find some of the right questions and answers along the way, these are the ingredients of maturity. Let's hope you're on the way *up!*

"The electric rim-spin
on our planet is much
beyond the adaptive
power of the human
population. The overall
speedup of transactions
creates vast depression
of body and spirit alike.
Drugs may seem to offer
a means of achieving the
necessary 'speed.' In
fact, however, a great
psychic depression has
occurred. . . ."

(Marshall McLuhan,
"Students in the
Seventies," *Campus
Call,* January, 1970)

10. Defiance, Drugs, and Doomsday

Should a person's future be ruined by one 'trip' or experience of smoking 'pot'?" asked seventeen-year-old Ricky. He is not on drugs but knows some teen-agers who use them for kicks.

To raise such a question is part of youth's curiosity, but drugs now arouse a hornet's nest of controversy. Observers say Ricky's question raises more issues, all subject to dispute: Is marijuana a drug of "psychic dependence"? Does it cause "psychotic episodes" (make you crazy) or brain damage? How does "Mary Jane" influence motor skills, like driving an automobile, and artistic creativity? Answers are biased, according to one's conservative-liberal-radical style of life.

Many parents of teen-agers do not sleep well. Besides the traditional fears of drinking, reckless driving, premarital sex, urban riots, war, and sudden death at the hands of a mad gunman, there is now the narcotics nightmare.

When the underground poets, like Allen Ginsberg and Lawrence Ferlinghetti (*A Coney Island of the Mind*), finished their missionary work a decade ago, America's youth felt liberated. Adolescent defiance—the disposition to challenge, oppose, and resist the status quo—was urged by the Timothy Leary boys as an expression of human empathy and individual freedom. Psychedelic discovery, promising insightful trips into reality, has spread far and wide—into black slums and rich white suburbs. We have also discovered that kicks have kickbacks.

Younger and younger teen-agers, along with many eleven- and twelve-year-olds, are inhaling, swallowing, and injecting an astonishing array of chemical substances. *Life* stated (February 20, 1970) that there are an estimated 20,000 teen-age heroin addicts in New York City alone. Thousands die of heroin overdoses each year. And hundreds of thousands of your fellow students are experimenting with marijuana, LSD, and other chemicals. Drug abuse is reaching epidemic proportions.

Talking or Taking?

"Sure, I turn on every two or three weeks. I've never had any trouble when I turn on. It makes me feel good in an excited-all-over sort of way. I like to be around people when I'm high. I laugh, enjoy people, and accept them as they are. My friends can all tell when I'm high. They enjoy my company as much then as at other times." [33]

This description of some effects of marijuana comes from a minister's son, with a solid B standing, who is not angrily protesting against parents. He looks cleancut and would never be mistaken for the hippie-type rebel.

Some teen-agers take, others talk, about the mind-benders. Many experiment once or twice and quit. Others continue and get hooked. The surge of student suicides—blamed on grades, the war, fear of a nuclear holocaust, and sex—may be linked, in part, to the predicament of drug dependency.

Forbidden fruit is always the sweetest, goes the old adage. There is an allure, a mysterious appeal, of drugs on the teen-age scene. You hear rumors of a weekend pot party at a friend's lake cabin while her parents were in Denver on a business trip. Somebody who hasn't used drugs turns on once, then reports a delightful sensation. Damage appears minor, feelings appear happier, until—until the daughter of a celebrity like Art Linkletter leaps to her death, until her father explains that she could not cope with reality as a teen-age divorcee and was on LSD.

You know the quaint vocabulary kids sling around. They talk about drugs as much to frighten, at least irritate, their elders as anything. You may be curious about drug talk.

The amphetamines or stimulants are known as "Bennies, Crystals, Co-Pilots, Dexies, Drivers, Footballs, Hearts, Oranges, Peaches, Pep Pills, Roses, and Wake Ups." The barbiturates or sedatives are known as "Blue Heavens, Candy, Devils, Double Trouble, Downs, Peanuts, Phennies, Purple Hearts, Red Devils, and Yellow Jackets."

LSD (Lysergic Acid Diethylamide), the consciousness expanding psychedelic which promises "instant paradise," is also called "Acid, Big D, Chief, Cubes, Hawk, Sugar, Twenty-Five, and Trips." Marijuana, a milder hallucinogen, is actually a depressant (intoxicant) like alcohol. It is also known as "Gage, Grass, Hay, Hemp, Jive, Mary Jane, Mezz, MU, Muggles, Pot, Rope, Tea, and Weed." Marijuana cigarettes are called "Joints, Sticks, or Reefers." High-grade marijuana is called "Manicure." The addictive drug heroin, an opiate, is referred to as "Dope, Hard Stuff, Harry, H., Horse, Junk, Scat, Smack, and Snow." So goes the jargon.

The fifteen-year-old daughter of an engineer came home from

high school one day with this report: "Some girls were in the rest room today spraying hair spray into paper bags; then they were getting high inhaling the stuff." Wow! Was her mother ever bugged by that scary tale.

To get high, some kids will try almost anything. They swallow pills, sniff glue, inhale fumes, and gulp cough syrup. They are blind to any danger, and deaf to grownup's warnings. "We want to live today; tomorrow may never come," is the going argument. It sends parents into spasms.

"Why do they desire stuff like that?" you wonder. "Why do kids get mixed up with drugs, live a day-to-day existence, steal, shoplift, or sell dope in order to buy drugs themselves?"

A twenty-one-year-old plainclothes agent grew a beard, joined a colony of drug users in a city park, and reported his undercover findings. "They want anything that will give them a buzz. If they can't get what you might call 'regular drugs' then they'll shoot anything—Dristan, cough medicine or anything with a drug label on it. . . . There was one guy who loved the needle. I've watched him shoot up with heroin and he'd shoot a little bit and then pull the needle out of his arm. He'd wait awhile and shoot some more. He loved that needle. He would stick it in and out of his arm.

"Then there were the little twelve- and thirteen-year-old girls who would come down to the park because they thought it was cool and the people they met there were 'free.' Really, they were all mad at their parents. Most of them had problems with their parents—some were too lax and some were too strict."

What's Behind Drug Involvement?

There's a lot of misinformation going around about drug use and abuse. Some journalists prefer sensationalism, make the "hard stuff" appear cool, and the addict a culture hero to juveniles. Movies, picturing ecstacy and peace, and avoiding the terror and temporary psychotic episodes induced by hallucinogens, demoralize rather than help young people to cope intelligently with chemical crutches.

An Albuquerque housewife reported the dangers of mis-education among parents, teachers, and concerned youth (*Life,* March 13, 1970). Here is her warning against confusing ad-vice: "We attended a PTA meeting on drug abuse that: tended to confuse all drugs with heroin; refused to include alcohol as a dangerous drug; thrilled over endless, sensational anti-kid stories; pictured a pusher as a bearded fellow with rolling eyes; emphasized detection techniques—going through drawers, test-ing eyes; advised frightening the kids and 'showing authority.'

"The parents cheered the sadistic-masochistic interplay that produces the tragedy in the first place. As a result of the advice given at this meeting, friends of ours have arranged to take their sons (the oldest is twelve) to the city jail to watch a junkie suffer withdrawal."

You need to check the source of your data thoroughly. Thoughtful persons are giving their lives in the study and pre-vention of drug abuse. Others offer a hoax, witchcraft, and bad news that worries but fails to inform intelligent citizens. "Who says?" is a better response than "You don't say!" Skepticism should lead cautious teen-agers, not to escapism, but to discover the truth. Since drugs offer a shaky ship for life's uncertain voyage, why do kids get high?

One man who has made a lengthy study of this problem is UCLA psychiatrist J. Thomas Ungerleider, M.D. He cited seven reasons for youth's involvement: [34]

Curiosity about drugs, engendered by our adult drug cul-ture—including tobacco (nicotine), coffee (caffeine), alcohol, tranquilizers, diet pills, sleeping pills, and pep pills—advertised everywhere.

Peer group pressure. It is almost becoming a puberty rite to have experimented with drugs by the time you are fourteen or fifteen. It is one of the most talked-about subjects today.

Affluence and permissiveness. Bored teen-agers with a car, money, and no responsibilities or meaningful work opportunities have plenty of opportunity to experiment with drugs. Tom, featured in *Life,* "Heroin in the High Schools" (February 20,

1970) said that his parents did not know of his addiction. Drug use can be hidden temporarily.

Rebelliousness. Kids see drugs as a way to get their parents or teachers "uptight"—frightened or anxious.

Instant acceptability. Kids think they can create an identity by getting involved in the drug scene; its easier than long hours of study or athletic practice.

Psychedelics such as marijuana and LSD can *dampen internal conflicts and insecurities* (and prevent coming to grips with them) without losing consciousness, as one does with sleeping pills or too much alcohol. But it is the very struggle with these feelings that leads to maturity and emotional growth.

Finally, some young people use drugs *just "for kicks."*

"But what about an opinion from someone who has actually tried it, not a medical or antipsychedelic stance," you ask. You are right. Aldous Huxley wrote in *The Doors of Perception* (*bound with Heaven and Hell*): [35] "This is how one ought to see, how things really are." While under the influence of mescaline Huxley claimed to be in intense touch with reality.

In an address to the New York Academy of Sciences, in 1957, Huxley predicted that pharmacologists would provide human beings a path to peace, perception, and instant joy. "If we want beauty, they will . . . open the door to visions of unimaginable riches and significance. If our desire is for life everlasting, they will give us the next best thing: Eons of blissful experience miraculously telescoped into a single hour."

Huxley's predictions proved only half true. While hallucinogenic drugs can induce "a return to Eden where I could lose all my worries and imagine many things," as a West Coast student said, they can also bring the terror of temporary insanity. Once trips are taken, flashbacks may occur six months later producing psychotic episodes in apparently normal students.[36]

Opinions vary as to physical effects of these drugs. LSD "does not seem to either stimulate or diminish sexual drive," says one medical report. There is some evidence that it may damage human chromosomes. Teen-age users risk birth defects in their offspring. A recent study showed that chronic marijuana users get the same high smoking joints lacking the actual "grass" ingredient as they did with real marijuana. Thus, some perceptions and distortions are self-induced. A teen-ager who enjoys life may experience a good trip. If you're depressed and smoke pot, you're likely to get more depressed. A suicidal student gets more suicidal. Such news cannot be viewed lightly. Your life is at stake.

"Can kids who've tried it quit or is there no place to go once you've started turning on?" Some students who had tried marijuana and LSD answered in an anonymous questionnaire.

"I have stopped taking drugs. . . . It became too easy to 'groove' on something . . . without ever coming to terms with real problems, without ever really thinking. The borders of illusion and reality became hazy. . . ."

An older adolescent wrote: "I consider it now a part of the growing up process. It was an answer. It no longer is. I am still overwhelmed by the madness that is my country, but I must find another way of coming to terms with it."

You probably know that friends are smoking marijuana and haven't flipped out or are still making good grades. You may be tempted to try it yourself. Before seeking escape in drugs, consider the possible emptiness after the party's over.

The Baylor Lariat (March 11, 1970, page 2) takes you to an imaginary pot party. Here's a student's view of "The Experimenters." Imagine yourself joining a tight circle.

Chords of blasting, searching acid rock engulfing the room. . . . People . . . nervous, as he unwraps the plastic bag.

They all come from good families. But curiosity about the grass that can put them away for five years has moved them to roll their own. Just so much, enough for them to find out whether it is as good or bad as they say. . . .

The yellow and blue flame touches the end of the joint, igniting it, but quickly changes to a reddish-orange glow. He sucks the swirling smoke down to the base of his lungs. Holding it there, closing his eyes and leaning forward, he passes it to her. . . .

Around the circle it is passed . . . once . . . twice, and it is gone, burned to the point where fingers can no longer hold it.

Still there is a feeling of expectancy, but not fulfillment. Nothing has happened except a certain lightness of the head. They must try again.

The plastic bag comes back out. The ritual is performed. This time she does not cough, but begins laughing. Uncontrollable laughter. Another does the same, while some look on, amused, but not sharing the same feeling.

They move away from the crowd . . . . They touch each other, look, stare. They see for the first time their minds heightened, but still controlled. They close their eyes, all but the laughing girl, who can't stop. . . .

He rewraps the stuff and replaces it in the cache, where no living nark could find it. They will remain there for several more hours, until either sleep or reality overtakes them. They will think about it then. Some will not enjoy the experience, and others will come again to undo the plastic bag.

Perspectives on a Complex Problem

Statistics are less plentiful than hearsay. In your town, on your campus, the drug problem may be small. But, in some schools, up to 50 percent of the students have experimented with dope. The general public fears the hard-core user, alienates and arrests (when possible) professional drug pushers. Some one-time experimenters, once they are caught, can face legal action—anywhere from a two-year probated sentence to life in prison.

A bunch of guys and gals you know may have tried it. You alone can't stamp out marijuana or LSD, but you can try to deal intelligently with it when it comes your way. Here are three perspectives on drugs to help you face street-corner myths.

Medical.—Stanley Yolles, M.D., former director, National Institute of Mental Health, answers teen questions.[37] To quote:

> *Is it safe to try drugs once just to see how it feels?*
> This depends entirely upon the drug and the person—both of which involve important unknown quantities. Few people

who try heroin once, for example, never touch it again. On the other hand, a majority of people who try marijuana . . . do so fewer than 10 times before quitting entirely.

You cannot be certain ahead of time of your own reaction to a drug experience. About 10 percent of the people who try marijuana . . . become chronic, compulsive users, often to their surprise. Some drugs, such as LSD and . . . 'speed' can cause serious harm even with one experimental dosage.

Conclusion? The risks of any kind of drug taking are too great to be dismissed lightly.

Can I become addicted to "pot?"

Marijuana does not cause addiction . . . . But it can be as habit-forming as ordinary cigarettes. Chronic users become dependent upon it psychologically. Without it, they may feel restless, unable to face life.

What should I do at a party where everyone is on drugs and they're trying to get me to take them?

Leave immediately! Most people start on drugs the first time in just such circumstances. Even if you stay but don't "turn on," you are in danger legally. A person present where drugs are being used can be arrested along with the users.

Isn't marijuana safer than alcohol?

We have much yet to learn about the long-range effects of marijuana . . . . Both intoxicants can impair your physical coordination and hamper your judgment.

Will using "pot" lead to other drugs?

Most occasional marijuana smokers never "progress" to stronger substances. But heavy, regular users (or "potheads") often do. These people are likely to be emotionally disturbed and seem to have a basic need to try other drugs.

What can happen during a "bad trip" on LSD?

Almost anything. The sense of losing control during hallucinations can cause you to panic and blindly injure yourself or others . . . . Because of feelings of omniscience and indestructibility, the "tripper" may believe he can fly—and plunge to his death from a high window as many have done.

Is it true that "speed" kills?

Some medical authorities estimate that once you become

hooked on "speed" your life expectancy is about five years. Besides the risk of brain damage, habitual use takes a heavy toll on the user's liver and heart.

Can I become addicted to "medicine chest" drugs?

Definitely. In fact, many young people are getting "high" illicitly on the very drugs their parents use under prescription.

Can a person stop using drugs by himself?

Once you are addicted or habituated to drugs, it is very unlikely that you can "cure" yourself. In some cases, deep-seated psychological or character disorders, which require psychiatric treatment, may lie behind drug-taking. An abrupt withdrawal from some drugs is dangerous. For these reasons, hospitalization or at least close professional supervision while kicking the drug habit is most desirable.

Legal.—United States legal codes are not uniform concerning drug offenses. In Texas, for example, the sale or possession of LSD is only a misdemeanor, while marijuana is a felony. In some states smoking pot might bring only misdemeanor charges. State statutes classify drug offenses in two categories—possession and sale. First offense *possession* of marijuana, in Texas, is punishable by not less than two years and not more than life in prison. Punishment for its *sale* can go as high as life but not lower than ten years.

"Sale" in the Texas statutes, according to attorney Ken Crow of McLennan County, covers a wide variety of acts. A person who trades, barters, gives, sells or even offers to undertake any of these acts can be charged with sale of marijuana.

As in most felony cases, someone convicted of possession who has never been convicted of a felony in the United States is eligible for a probated sentence if the sentence is less than ten years. Eligibility does not assure that he will get probation however.

Moot questions arise over drug use. Sociologist Erich Goode, editor of a major study entitled *Marijuana* (Atherton Press, 1969), discovered an agglomeration of different attitudes in American life. Members of varied political and professional groups see drugs the way they view the rest of the universe—on a conservative-liberal-radical scale. Some opt for relaxed laws, particularly concerning marijuana possession. Others think laws should be strengthened or at least made uniform.

Marijuana, noted Goode, is "a kind of *symbol* for a complex of other positions, beliefs and activities which are correlated with and compatible with its use." [38] In other words, people who use marijuana are viewed by nonusers as moral liberals who likely engage in loose sexual practices, have a dim view of patriotism, and attack the Establishment at the drop of any issue. Drug users live dangerously by violating the belief systems, as well as state statutes, of millions of Americans.

Personal.—I have faced many temptations through the years —revenge toward someone or the system itself, to retreat from life's rough spots, to resist social change. But drug use has never been my cup of tea. I feel sorry for any teen-ager tricked into trusting the wrong things, because I have been fooled and hurt myself by men greedy for power or a fast buck. And I do not like to be taken advantage of by anyone!

In my judgment, some things are best never begun. "Drugs for kicks" is one of those things you can avoid with profit. There are enough worries over the draft, sex, grades, parents, acne, overweight, loneliness, alcohol—myriads of other problems— that it's depressing to add drugs to the list.

Curiosity may have already gotten the best of you. Maybe you did not know who to believe. If you're already a "tripper" and want to stop, where do you go for help? Read a book on the weed of death, move to Mexico, kill yourself? Hardly!

Turn to someone you trust—a teacher, parent, doctor, friend —and ask him to help you locate the best professional help available in your community or area of the state. Mixed-up feelings may have turned you to drugs in the first place. You cannot unmix them alone. The cure rate for drug users is discouraging—another good reason not to get involved.

"No" is your final freedom. Use it when you need to.

> "Plan now for the future
> in case there is one."
>
> (Sign in a New York
> shop window)

11. When Things Get You Down

"I wonder if I'm ever going to make my goal because there are so many hells around me." The attractive seventeen-year-old girl who said that was experiencing more than a "bad day." She was moody, discouraged, facing frustrating problems that left her depressed. Her parents were splitting up; she was caving in.

Have you ever wondered, "Why must we go through such a baffling world in order to get to heaven?" If so, you're more human than otherwise. It's a common question.

Lucy, of the famed Schulz comic strip *Peanuts,* talked once about life's "ups" and "downs."

LUCY: Sometimes I get discouraged.

CHARLIE BROWN: Well, Lucy, life does have its ups and downs, you know . . . .

LUCY: But why? Why *should* it?! Why can't my life be all *"ups"?* If I want all "ups," why can't I have them? Why can't I just move from one "up" to another "up"? . . . . I don't want any "downs"! I just want "ups" and "ups" and "ups"!

CHARLIE BROWN: I can't stand it . . . .

Life, like the weather, is made of extremes. You are either encouraged—eager about some idea or project—or discouraged. You feel great or sick about a biology exam, for which you had studied three hours. You're ready to tackle things or you're ready to give up. Skies are blue, then a teacher "has it in" for you. Suddenly, your best friend moves or there's a big fight at home, and you feel threatened, insecure.

Most people have troubles at least once in a while. Some people have a load of worries that may weigh them down.

Girls seem to experience bigger mood swings—"upper-ups" and "lower-lows"—than boys. Personality patterns point boys toward activities, sports achievements, and work experiences, and girls toward more passive reflection. The female tends to be sensitive, preoccupied with relationships, which leads ultimately to the development of "feminine intuition." Guys tend to bump blindly through rough spots, whereas, girls tend to withdraw, perhaps cry, and talk things over with a friend.

A lot of fantasy thinking goes on among all teen-agers. Sometimes your imagination (dark thoughts) gets you in trouble.

After a romantic quarrel, a sixteen-year-old girl said, "I find that since I have been unsuccessful in love I no longer want to share love with another person. How can I increase my capacity for love?" Meanwhile, her boyfriend shot basketball goals two or three days after school and felt better. He wasn't as spellbound by their dating encounters as she was.

Trouble hits teen-agers, too, not just Washington, D. C. or the Middle East. Some things happen beyond your control.

Crises Beyond Your Control

Did you happen to see Stanley Kubrick's *2001: A Space Odyssey?* The movie pictures man's coming struggle with machines in the twenty-first century of space exploration. If the film has a hero, it is space: the stars, planets, and unbelievable distances between earth and interstellar matter.

Man—Machines.—You are not responsible for the dramatic struggle between the United States and Russia to place men on far-flung planets. You must survive, however, in a new galactic ecology.

In *2001,* man takes a back seat to technology and its conflicts with alien environments. Picturing man's beginnings, two hordes of gorillas open the "story" by fighting over a waterhole. Almost too quickly, the film leaps to A.D. 2001 with a spaceship approaching a satellite port. A story emerges within a story as a flight leaves for Jupiter. The crew members take orders from a programmed computer, a genius named Hal. Eventually, there is a struggle. Distrust builds up between a crew member, Dave, and Hal to the point of Dave's unscrewing Hal's memory banks. The computer is reduced to a stuttering idiot; man and machine have been alienated. Have you noticed how many human jobs machines can do? Does it worry you?

Thermonuclear weapons.—After the shocking bombings of Hiroshima and Nagasaki, Japan, some United States physicists wanted to uninvent the A-bomb. You have suppressed your terror over the Bomb, but movies like *Fail-Safe* and *The War Game* remind you of man's utter helplessness in the grips of atomic destruction.

Political revolutions.—The movement toward a new America is underway. Dissent (like draft resisters) and violence (like the armed student take-over at Cornell) are common. Still, the United States government system is stable in comparison to

Cuba and South American revolts. I asked a teen-age refugee from Cuba what life was like after Castro changed things. He capsuled history in three words: "Things got tougher." Is anarchy or cooperative effort the way to a new America?

Accidents.—Accidents can happen so quickly. You say goodbye to your mother and dad, join your friends in a car pool for school, then someone runs a stop sign!

"I thought the other car was gonna stop, Mom," explained Bobby. "It was an old man and his wife. We had the right of way, but they just kept comin' and slammed into us."

Your little sister enjoys swinging on the school playground during recess or free playtime. Then, one day, a guy runs up to you in the hall and asks if you've heard that your sis fell from a swing, has a brain concussion, and is waiting in the nurse's office for an ambulance.

If you're a normal guy, you like to play ball. Once in a great while, a baseball flies out of reach and through somebody's plate glass door or window. It may be simple—an inexpensive windowpane; it may be a complex—a costly sliding door replacement. In any case, you need to admit your involvement in the game and bear your share of the expense.

Suffering.—An earthquake wipes out a whole village. A ski resort disappears under a snow slide and forty vacationers are killed. A jet liner over shoots a runway, belly lands in a nearby lake, and twenty-three lives are lost. There are accidental killings even in wartime. A United States Cobra helicopter fires three rockets into the wrong crowd—American soldiers—ten are killed and thirteen men injured by mistake!

And so it goes. There is social unrest, urban uprisings, black-white showdowns over housing or schools. As long as it's *them,* it doesn't sting so much. But when it's *us*—one of us is hurt, has a heart attack, is assaulted or robbed—it's serious.

You can't help it if cancer kills the mother of your best friend, if blacks riot in Detroit, if your little brother is a mongoloid child. Some crises are beyond your control. Your attitude toward such things *is* your responsibility. On the other hand, you help some things to go wrong.

What About Your Hang-Ups?

Your biggest problem right now may be an internal crisis, one of your own making. You may be hung-up over a poor attitude toward persons in authority, anger, guilt, or some questionable habit. Let's illustrate.

Authority, freedom, and responsibility.—Interpersonal relations make you uniquely *you*. Not all ties with others are pleasant as you grow up and demand more freedom.

Letting go of parents who have provided for your every need for eighteen or more years is only half the problem. They must let go of you, too, if you're free at last.

"I told my daughter that, when she married, she was on her own; I was through," reflected a middle-aged father. "But I was dead wrong. It was one of the biggest boo-boos of my life." Though Jan was grown and married, she still needed her father and mother as friends and, occasionally, as financial helpers.

As you become "your own man," or woman, you'll level with parents, school principals, police officers, pastors, priests, or rabbis. You'll learn that life has rules and regulations for all ages of people; that they apply to you. Some matters—like car use or later dating privileges—must be negotiated. As you show responsibility, more freedom comes. At least it should.

Anger.—"I'm so mad at that old bag I could spit!" said Emily on the way home from school one afternoon. "She keeps piling on the algebra homework without grading our papers and telling us the right answers."

Change the setting. You and your sister are talking about a letter she received from Bill at Camp Pendleton. You try to see the message, but she jerks her letter away: "It's none of your business!" For some unexplainable reason, you are madder than mad about her secret love life with Bill.

One other incident. An eighteen-year-old boy is driving the

family car on vacation. He gets the wheel from his father after a rest stop and expects to drive a couple of hours until noon. His sister, a sixteen-year-old who recently completed a driver's education course, asks to drive. The pattern goes like this— request, pester, torment, threaten, then attack the older brother. Finally, Joe says, "What do you expect me to do?" And his sister snaps, "You give me a pain in the neck!" Wow!

Hostility happens in the best (as well as the worst) of families. Sometimes, your mother or dad will explode, lash out, misunderstand your motives, or accuse you unjustly. You will be terribly hurt. But what can you do?

Everybody gets mad; you're not the author of that. Two points are pivotal: (1) awareness of anger in life situations, and (2) deciding how to use anger. These are both your obligations. Uncontrollable rage is risky. Did you ever see a child throw a temper tantrum—clench his fists and have a "conniption fit"? Automatic anger in a temperamental person racks his whole body. You've seen the symptoms in a high-strung person: the body shakes, face flushes, blood boils, voice quivers. He blows his top, is not like himself, and you flare up protectively in return.

Nature provides us with defenses against attacks. We can deliberately decide what to say or do in a given set of circumstances, or fly off the handle. It's wiser to handle a frontal attack—something that makes you mad—with direct, yet careful, conversation than to hit the ceiling. The more in control you are, the healthier your disposition of the hurt.

For example, if you are put out with someone, say: "We're not getting anywhere. Got any clues?"

When parents force teen-agers to cap off and bottle upset feelings, they teach the dishonesty of suppression. Sooner or later, anyone who loses face or swallows temper is in trouble. Either physical symptoms—like crying, getting a headache, or ulcers—occur or revenge takes its deadly toll.

You need to develop healthy ways of coping with everyday,

garden variety anger. Holding hatred, like a deep breath, is impossible. One can become temporarily insane, do dangerous things—like attacking someone physically or with a gun—until rage is resolved. Depression, self-punishment for feeling (but not honestly expressing) anger, is hypocrisy's price tag.

The Bible suggests that we are to speak the truth in love. This means you need diplomacy, tact, and compassion in order to express anger in nondestructive ways. It's no sin to feel irritated inside, but to hold hatred and seek revenge toward another person is wrong. We all need to learn the power of forgiveness.

Guilt.—"Yes, I believe that God can forgive me," said the eighteen-year-old girl who had spent a weekend fling in a boyfriend's apartment, "but I can't ever forgive myself. I'm ruined." She also feared that her counselor would reject her.

How often have you felt like that? No teen-ager is loyal to all of his loyalties all of the time. You step over the boundary, even of your self-styled code of ethics, not one imposed by others like dorm rules on campus. The more sensitive your conscience, the greater your suffering and self-punishment when values are violated.

"Americans," said psychiatrist Robert R. Rynearson, "need a value system for all seasons." What does that mean? It suggests:

1. Relationships are superior to rules in making a go of life. Enduring principles like love and justice, not codes, support human life.

2. Relationships may be disrupted by anger, betrayal of trust, absence, indifference, dishonesty, indecency, and violence. Self-centeredness, what the Bible calls pride and psychiatry calls narcism, is the seedbed of ruined relationships.

3. Rationalizing by denying guilt feelings prevents absolution. You cannot live with unresolved feelings of guilt.

4. Relationships are restored by forgiveness, not by buying back God's or another's love. Once we have accepted another's acceptance of us, we are freed for responsible living again.

Coping with Your Problems

Think it over. You probably have a system figured out for meeting your frustrations. There are healthy and unhealthy ways to escape life's pressures.

I don't know your specific difficulty—not enough money; your parents distrust you; your sister's too bossy; that special friendship is not working out; hypocrisy with you and those around you. Some problems are little, like having to wash the dishes or mow the front lawn. Some anxieties, like a broken engagement with the person you were to marry, are much greater.

Try to be honest as you answer these questions.

Are you going around looking for trouble? Life at best is risky business. You don't have to look for trouble. It looks for you and will find you. Nobody enjoys a trouble-maker.

Have you complied with adult (or legal) precautions? If, for example, your parents have requested that you not travel the 350 miles home from college in a friend's Volkswagon (for safety's sake), did you listen? If you've been cautioned against parking in a high-crime area of the city, did you invite your date home after the late movie? If it is a good idea not to lend a lot of money to other kids, or borrow from them, will conflicts arise if you lend or borrow money?

Do you have a friend or counselor who is trained to help you understand yourself and your problem? There are times when you run into issues or crises that are too big to handle. True, you may want to be alone temporarily, but call for help when you need it. Give your parents a chance to try to help you. Why hide secrets? Most parents will do what they can to help.

Do "bad days" come along once in a while for everyone? You get a headache. Your stomach hurts. You lose a lot of sleep. You fail a test or don't have a social studies assignment. Physical feelings can have a big effect on your emotions. Luckily, bad days don't last forever. So this is a bad day! You're cross and irritable. Tomorrow, things will be better.

Can you change, delay, or revise your goal in light of life's realities? Perhaps you want a motorcycle, a new dress, or something that appears impossible. Your parents are against it. You may not have enough money saved for that big purchase. Perhaps you aimed too high—wanted all A's—and have a grade card that looks like a roller-coaster, with high and low grades. Some people, like Martin Luther King, rationalize "why we can't wait." If you are prone to live recklessly then accept the consequences.

Have you learned anything from your losses? Troubles have a way of turning around and befriending us to keep us out of more trouble later. Date-trouble with one boy can teach you what to avoid next time you're out with a fellow. If blowing up with your dad or a teacher has created "bad news," what will help you control your temper?

Have you forgiven persons who hurt you, and accepted the forgiveness of someone you offended? One of the clues to Jesus Christ's helpful life was his daily living of forgiveness. Rather than worrying about something, or taking yourself too seriously, forget it or work to improve the situation.

Are you releasing pent-up emotions through productive work and relaxing play? Clean up your room, take a hike, listen to music, do push-ups. It's amazing what exercise and fun can do.

Problems come to everyone. Some crises are beyond your control. Discovering ways to get on top of your troubles will set the direction of your life. With God's help, you can.

"Man moves toward
health and salvation. . . .
Religion says there's
always a chance to
become creative. There
is always something
growing in human
beings with which you
can make an alliance."

(Case conference
seminar, psychiatrist
Robert S. Glen, M.D.)

12. Moving Toward Maturity

A tiny New York harbor tugboat piloted an ocean-going vessel from its berth at dockside to the open sea. The tug's pilot, as a final salute, beamed this message to the ship's captain: "You're on your own now." That is my salute to you.

Throughout these discussions one assumption has run like a golden thread: it's tough growing up. One thing for sure, being a teen-ager today is no bore. That you are facing life's transitions with courage and candor is a great encouragement to parents like me. Soon, you will be an adult decision-maker, on your own. The world will say, "It's up to you now."

I have assumed that you possess the ingredients essential for human growth:

That you inherited a healthy mind and body at birth.

That you received proper upbringing, plenty of love and sufficient discipline, from your parents.

That you have experienced "normal" life processes and count yourself an average American teen-ager.

That, if hang-ups (unhealthy emotional patterns) persist you have access to skilled help to correct such problems.

That's quite an assumption—really a compliment to you and your childhood family—since many adults remain immature. Hopefully, then, you are the growing kind, and have been freed by responsible adults around you to grow to your full potential.

What Is Maturity?

A young friend asked me: "Is there such a thing as reaching maturity? It seems that life is a process of maturing and that the older adult has not reached full maturity." Do you agree?

Maturity is a term that has been used in various ways. The adjective "mature" comes from the Latin *maturus,* meaning "ripe," according to Webster's *New Collegiate Dictionary.* In modifying the noun "person," *mature* implies a quality, state, or condition of full development. It presupposes a life-long growth process called maturation. The emerging dynamic self—your own unique personality—grows through several stages. Despite ups and downs, slow periods and fast spurts, you grow as a male or female being.

Yes, all living things—cells, tissues, organisms—are born to grow. Wine, after a fermentation period, is said to reach a desired state of perfection (maturity). Trees push upward in the forest; flowers surge skyward on the mountainside. Animals terminate growth when full physical development comes. Man, unique in all creation, keeps growing in outlook, ideas, data, and insights until death. The life cycle is then complete.

Growing up is not just physical—marking off notches on grandmother's pantry door to see if you're six feet tall. *Human growth is total, and maturing is a life-long process.* It includes your social context, economic circumstances, parental willingness both to love and grant you independence, your sexuality, sense of values, life goals, educational opportunities, motives, and grasp of reality.

For our purposes we shall interpret *maturity* to mean the full development of all resources to capacity for a given age. A five-year-old child may be mature if all his or her resources are developed as much as they could be at age five. A seventeen-year-old person is mature, physically and in outlook, if all resources of body, mind, and spirit are developed to full capacity for seventeen years.

You know how boys and girls test themselves to reassure transitions toward adolescence. Boys try physical feats of performance or endurance, like jumping across a creek or jumping across apartment building roofs in the city. Girls play like women by dressing in long frocks and walking in high-heels. Both sexes check body development for signs of puberty, like body hair and emerging breasts. Youths also have their own standards for becoming a man or woman. Some teenage growth criteria are appropriate, others unhealthy or unwise. "Proving one's manhood" among some groups can be too risky and costly.

"What about immaturity?" you wonder. Perhaps you know adults with so many hang-ups from adolescence that they have a terrible time in life. What shall we say of the twenty-year-old who still throws a tantrum like a two-year-old?

No individual develops all his potential resources to full capacity at a given time. Human growth is uneven, not smooth. Different persons develop at different rates and degrees. You, at fifteen, may be lagging behind in mental development while enjoying phenomenal physical growth. Someone you know is way ahead of you socially—already dating, entering talent contests, or performing as an artist in public. You may be shy, feel terribly lonely, yet be his or her age. This difference need not alienate you from the group, but you may have to try a bit harder to be more outgoing with others.

Each age makes its own demands, requires certain tasks be performed, from the cradle to the grave. Maturity at age forty is more demanding than maturity at age eighteen. Still, an eighteen-year-old person faces tremendous challenges in growing up. One needs a healthy, joyous adolescent period as a launch-pad into adulthood.

Because growth is always in process, you can speak of maturing (not fully mature) people. Some of your friends are more mature than others. Some cling to selfish baby ways, making excessive demands on adults, too long. The goal of growth is maturity—a healthy, fully-functioning, free, growing person. That's what this book has been about.

Growing Up Free

A common adolescent complaint is: "What gives parents and teachers the idea that pressuring a young person will help him 'find himself'? They push off many unnecessary responsibilities on us. Don't we need more time just to get to know ourselves?" The other side of that plea for "more time" is your desire for instant adulthood—with all the privileges and freedoms that maturity implies.

Young people are like tender plants. You need healthy conditions (warm concern, nourishment, protection, light and fresh air) and freedom to unfold in your own way. Parents cannot *make* their young grow up at an adult rate of speed. They can only provide the conditions for a teen-ager to progress into an independent, responsible, and productive citizen.

It's hard for parents to let go their children's hands and see them walking independently away. Your mother scolds regressive behavior, like an unkempt room or tardy lessons. Your dad tends to keep everything as smooth, cozy, and comfortable as possible—to put a false face of stability on social upheaval, hurts, and changes. Sooner or later, the masks come down and you discover the not-so-quiet desperation your parents face as you sail through school. It's tough for them, too.

Your dad gets transferred. If he keeps his job with the company where he's built ten years of seniority, you must move to Chicago or Tulsa or Charlotte. Schools are different, people are different, and you bitterly blame your father for moving. Remember, when you feel at your uncooperative worst, he didn't choose to move. He had to or start over with a new firm.

Some parents try to run their kids' risks for them. To quote a Rye, New York, father, with teen-age sons at Penn State and Duke: [39] "Any curious youngster at some point in high school or college is going to experiment a little—they always have. But what's lying around for grabs today is a little scary. . . . Wide-open sex, right on the campus, all kinds of drugs, Communist front groups that could blackmail you for life. My parents had to worry whether I'd get . . . suspended for breaking curfew. I have to worry whether my sons will disappear into some strange off-beat life before they ever know what they're leaving behind." See? Your risks are tougher.

By "growing up free" I imply *free* of neurotic hang-ups, of anxieties that can cripple you for life, not libertinism (immorality). Of course, your values are fluid, adaptable, and different from your parents' ideals. Yet, you need to be discriminating, selecting wisely from past and present beliefs, while forging a meaningful future.

So that you may test your growth against definite criteria of maturity, here are some characteristics which psychiatrists call "ideal." [40] How would you respond to these questions?

Am I relatively free of parasitic dependence upon my parents?

Can I relate to my parents constructively for their growth?

Is faith more a matter of caring relationships than keeping rules?

Can I risk myself in social relationships with others so that they sense I care for them, not just myself alone?

Do I accept my maleness or femaleness and live with mature sexual attitudes toward men and women?

Have I learned to discipline aggression (anger, hate, cruelty, revenge) so that my relationships are creative, not destructive? The mature adult is parental (loving) and creative, not infantile (demanding or destructive).

Do I possess a firm sense of reality, relatively free of distortions in outlook and prejudices against persons who are different from myself?

Am I future-oriented—trusting God, myself, others, and history —able to believe the best and optimistically to work for human betterment? Or am I anxious, mistrusting, guilty over childish impulses, and hung-up in the past?

Can I enjoy both celebrative play and responsible activities, and keep them in proper balance?

If your answer is "yes" to most of these standards of maturity and good mental health, you are lucky. Again, these are ideals. Few adults achieve full maturity. Most of us function in spite of blind spots, anxieties, and unhealthy defenses. We learn to accept ourselves and grow when possible.

"What about religious hang-ups like living on a treadmill?" you ask. In *How to be a Christian Without Being Religious* Fritz Ridenour exposes games like "playing church" and "purchasing fire insurance." He suggests that religious freedom comes, not in empty rules and rituals, but in response to God's gift in Christ.

Born to Move

Right now, you may not feel like you're taking hold of life. Though born to move ahead, pressures and problems may be pushing you backward. "I just can't concentrate except thinking about problems, daydreaming, and things of this nature," said a high school senior. His alcoholic mother had been institutionalized. Al suffered daily little dyings.

"How can I keep the growing edge (my healthy self) growing?" you wonder. My psychiatrist friend Robert Glen, M.D. said, "There is always something growing in human beings with which you can make an alliance." Think about it, for it's true.

Here is my own philosophy of growth to strengthen your move toward maturity. Even though you don't do the things you feel you should, and you've failed before, I shall assume the best about you.

I believe you desire maturity and will help life to happen for yourself and others around you. If so:

Keep growing from mistrust to faith.—Admit it. We are half-open people, suspicious of others, peering through the chinks in our armor. Someone's faith in me helps me find faith in myself. Another's love inspires my self-confidence. Once open to others, I risk myself—become vulnerable—like saying, "Hi, how are things going?" *first* for a change.

Keep growing from absence to being "there" with others.—Martin Buber, the late Jewish philosopher, called this moving from "I-it" to human "I-thou" relationships. When we're all wrapped up in our small, snug cocoons there's no room for people in our world. Life offers us daily chances to be present, not absent, with others: parents, teachers, friends.

Keep growing from phoniness to the courage of your own imperfections.—Nobody's perfect! People who wear masks, self-concealing phonies, fear honest self-revelation. Needing approval, fearing loss of face, they play the hypocrite game. If you dislike phoniness, you would agree with Jesus Christ who said to some men one day: Outwardly you look fine, but there's rotten stuff inside you (Matt. 23:28, free translation).

Carlyle Marney describes the "new holy man" in *The Coming Faith* (Abingdon, 1970) as anyone willing to obey God anywhere *in* the world. The challenge? "Will the real phony please stand up!"

Keep growing from despair to discovery.—Maybe you are sort of free, yet mostly stymied, in your situation. Your friends grow *up* while you just grow *older*. You want to change.

The common denominator in religious conversion and effective psychotherapy is *desire for change*. You will grow from the inside, not just taller, when you discover new growth patterns. If, for example, you need more privacy, go after it; don't just complain about the noise—try the library or tune out the radio. Encourage pushy parents to provide a private room.

Keep growing from holding grudges to forgiveness.—Hans Selye wrote in *The Stress of Life* that revenge kills more people than any other strong emotion. Some teen-agers are mad, hurt at what life has done to them. Others suffer guilt and remorse because of what they have done to life. In any case, it is costly to continue as a poor loser, with an ugly self-image, with destructive desires. New resolves, like, "Honest, Mom, I'll clean up my room every day." tend to fade. But practicing *and* receiving forgiveness, human and divine, is the turnpike toward maturity.

Keep growing from smugness to humble gratitude.—It's easy for a teacher to think he has "the word"; for a parent to feel that his word is "the law"; and a law enforcement officer to "play God." Both smug scientists and pompous ministers are tempted to think they "have it made." And an egotistical teen-ager can give all adults a hard time. You won't have to write a book on "My Humility and How I Achieved It" to develop gratitude. Just thank the powers that be for your great chance at life. Then don't "blow it"; be kind. Others also suffer.

Keep growing from anxiety to decisions for action.—You get a lot of data from your technological environment. The *soundaroundus* is deafening! TV, movies, newspapers, the *Playboy* philosophy, moon shots, politics, rumors, extremist's tactics. It's asking a lot to expect you to decode the information, then discard the "hogwash," all at age sixteen!

"What if I fail?" you ask. "There are so many decisions to make right now." To reply from my book *Dealing With Doubt* (Broadman Press, 1970): God calls for personal integrity but he does not demand perfection on earth. He expects his people to live faithfully with the light they have. His help, what the Bible calls "grace," sees us through. So, take hope.

Some wisdom from Harvey Cox's *The Feast of Fools* (Harvard University Press, 1969) should encourage you:

Christian hope suggests that man is destined for a City. It is not just any city, however. If we take the Gospel images as well as the symbols of the book of Revelation into consideration, it is not only a City where injustice is abolished and there is no more crying. It is a city in which a delightful wedding feast is in progress, where the laughter rings out, the dance has just begun, and the best wine is still to be served.

There is a larger, cosmic victory which, by faith, you can share. Meanwhile, get started! Keep moving toward maturity.

Psychiatrist Richard Huelsenbeck, M.D. moved back to his native Switzerland after living thirty-four years in New York City. In an article, "Reflections on Leaving America for Good," he answered his own question—Why? It was not disappointment; rather, "I left America because I felt I would never succeed in becoming an American in my heart." It's tough growing up. Hopefully, you will succeed in becoming a real person at heart. That is my earnest wish for you. All the best as you try!

Notes

[1] See, for example, Harmon L. Smith and Louis W. Hodges, *The Christian and His Decisions* (Nashville: Abingdon Press, 1969). Cf. E. G. Mesthene, *Technological Change* (Harvard Univ. Press, 1970).

[2] Walter Starcke, *The Ultimate Revolution* (New York: Harper & Row, 1969), p. 13.

[3] Kenneth Keniston, "Social Change and Youth in America," in *Youth: Change and Challenge*, edited by Erik H. Erikson (New York: Basic Books, Inc., 1963).

[4] Joseph B. Mow, "Jean-Paul Sartre: "Christian Theist?" *The Christian Century* (Nov. 23, 1966), 1437–39.

[5] Haim G. Ginott, *Between Parent and Teenager* (New York: The Macmillan Co., 1969), p. 30.

[6] Malcolm Boyd, *Are You Running With Me, Jesus?* (New York: Holt, Rinehart and Winston, Inc., 1965). Used by permission.

[7] Bob Oldenburg, *Happening Now* (Nashville: Broadman Press, 1969).

[8] Quoted by William V. Shannon, *The New York Times,* 1968.

[9] Erik H. Erikson, *Identity and the Life Cycle* (New York: International Universities Press, 1959).

[10] Abraham H. Maslow, *Toward a Psychology of Being,* 2d ed. (Princeton: D. Van Nostrand Co., Inc., 1968), p. 60.

[11] Evelyn M. Duvall, *About Sex and Growing Up* (New York: Association Press, 1968). Her *Love and the Facts of Life (Ibid.,* 1963) is a longer, more technical work for older adolescents.

[12] Quoted in Alvin Toffler, *Future Shock* (New York: Random House, 1970), pp. 86–87.

[13] Theodore Lidz, M.D., *The Person: His Development Throughout the Life Cycle* (New York: Basic Books, Inc., 1968), pp. 313–14.

[14] Charlie W. Shedd, *The Stork is Dead* (Waco, Texas: Word Books, 1968), p. 60.

[15] Quoted by Shedd, *Ibid.,* pp. 61–63.

[16] R. Lofton Hudson, *Persons in Crisis* (Nashville: Broadman Press,

1969), p. 24. See also Hudson's *Helping Each Other Be Human* (Waco, Texas: Word Books, 1970).

[17] See Rollo May, *Love and Will* (New York: W. W. Norton, 1969), p. 122 f.

[18] *Why Wait Till Marriage?* (New York: Association Press, 1965), pp. 112–15. Cf. John C. Howell, *Teaching About Sex* (Nashville: Broadman Press, 1966).

[19] William H. Grier and Price M. Cobbs, *Black Rage* (New York: Basic Books, Inc., 1968; Bantam ed., 1969), pp. 112–13.

[20] Eugene S. Wilson and Charles A. Bucher, *College Ahead!* (New York: Harcourt, Brace & World, Inc., 1961).

[21] The author is indebted to a team of psychiatrists and social workers who reported findings of a National Institute of Mental Health study, "Coping Strategies in a New Learning Environment," in Kaoru Yamamoto (ed.), *The College Student and His Culture: An Analysis* (Boston: Houghton Mifflin Company, 1968), pp. 331–44.

[22] Ernst Mayr, *Animal Species and Evolution* (Cambridge, Mass.: Harvard University Press, 1963).

[23] For a helpful introduction to human ecology, see Paul Shephard and Daniel McKinley (eds.), *The Subversive Science: Essays Toward An Ecology of Man* (Boston: Houghton Mifflin Co., 1969).

[24] Greenwich College Research Center, quoted in *The Baptist Student* (October, 1969), p. 43.

[25] John Fischer, "Survival U.: Prospectus for a really relevant University," *Harper's Magazine* (September, 1969), p. 12.

[26] See, for example, Joseph Katz, "The Student Activists: Rights, Needs, and Powers of Undergraduates," in *New Dimensions in Higher Education* (Washington: U. S. Office of Education, 1967); Block, Haan, and Smith, "Activism and Apathy in Contemporary Adolescents," in J. F. Adams (ed.), *Contributions to the Understanding of Adolescents* (Boston: Allyn and Bacon, 1967); Lawrence E. Dennis and Joseph F. Kauffman (eds.), *The College and the Student* (Washington: American Council on Education, 1966).

[27] "A Special Kind of Rebellion," *Fortune* (January, 1969), p. 68. Cf. Seymour M. Lipset, *Student Politics* (New York: Basic Books, Inc., 1967).

[28] Joseph Katz and Nevitt Sanford, "The New Student Power and Needed Reforms," in Kaoru Yamamoto (ed.) *The College Student and His Culture: An Analysis, op. cit.*, pp. 411–17.

[29] Quoted by Fischer, *op. cit.*, p. 12.

[30] David L. McKenna, "Protest Is No Plaything," *Action* (Summer, 1969), p. 14.

[31] See Nevitt Sanford, "The College Student of 1980," in Alvin C. Eurich (ed.) *Campus 1980: The Shape of the Future in American Higher Education* (New York: Delacorte Press, 1968), pp. 176–99.

[32] *The American Journal of Psychiatry* (August, 1969), p. 20. Cf. Mathew Ross, "Suicide Among College Students," *Ibid.*, pp. 220–25.

[33] Quoted by Charles Bowden, M.D. and Harold L. Wahking, "The Allure of Mary Jane," *The Baptist Student* (March, 1970), p. 34.

[34] Fort Worth Star-Telegram, January 4, 1970, p. 16–A.

[35] Huxley, (New York: Harper & Row Colophon, 1963), p. 34.

[36] Extensive research supported by NIMH has been conducted and reported by San Francisco psychiatrist Mardi J. Horowitz, M.D. "Flashbacks: Recurrent Intrusive Images After the Use of LSD," *American Journal of Psychiatry* (October, 1969), 565–69.

[37] Stanley Yolles, M.D., with Charles and Bonnie Remsberg, "An Expert Answers Teen-Agers' Questions About Drugs," *Family Weekly* (March 8, 1970), pp. 4–5.

[38] Sociologist Erich Goode, "Marijuana and the Politics of Reality," *Journal of Health and Social Behavior* (June, 1969), p. 92.

[39] George Barrett, *Fortune* (January, 1969), p. 92.

[40] Leon J. Saul, *Emotional Maturity: The Development and Dynamics of Personality* (Philadelphia: J. B. Lippincott Co., 2d ed., 1960), pp. 3–24.

Index of Names

Index of Subjects